# Living with the Nephilim the Seed of Destruction

# Living with the Nephilim the Seed of Destruction

**V. Bryan**

Copyright 2013

All rights reserved. No part of this publication may be reproduced without the prior permission of the publisher.
This book is protected by United States copyright laws.
Unless otherwise noted, Scripture reference in this book are taken from THE HOLY BIBLE, NEW INTERNATIONAL VERSION®, NIV® Copyright © 1973, 1978, 1984, 2011 by Biblica, Inc.™ Used by permission. All rights reserved worldwide.
Scripture quotations taken from the New American Standard Bible®, Copyright © 1960, 1962, 1963, 1968, 1971, 1972, 1973, 1975, 1977, 1995 by The Lockman Foundation Used by permission." (www.Lockman.org)
Scripture quotations marked (NLT) are taken from the Holy Bible, New Living Translation, copyright © 1996, 2004, 2007 by Tyndale House Foundation. Used by permission of Tyndale House Publishers, Inc., Carol Stream, Illinois 60188. All rights reserved.
"Scripture quotations taken from the Amplified® Bible, Copyright © 1954, 1958, 1962, 1964, 1965, 1987 by The Lockman Foundation Used by permission."
Scripture quotations marked "KJV" are taken from the Holy Bible, King James Version, Cambridge, 1769.
The Holy Bible, English Standard Version® (ESV®) Copyright © 2001 by Crossway, a publishing ministry of Good News Publishers.All rights reserved.
ESV Text Edition: 2007Scripture texts in this work are taken from the *New American Bible, revised edition* © 2010, 1991, 1986, 1970 Confraternity of Christian Doctrine, Washington, D.C. and are used by permission of the copyright owner. All Rights Reserved.
Scripture quotations are taken from the *Complete Jewish Bible*, copyright © 1998 by David H. Stern. Published by Jewish New Testament Publications, Inc. Distributed by Messianic Jewish Resources. www.messianicjewish.net. All rights reserved. Used by permission.
DARBY used under public domain.
Young's Literal Translation used under public domain.
American Standard Version of the Holy Bible used under public domain.

V Ly Publishing
Nephilim Imprint Books
1046 Church Rd, W 106-224
Southaven, MS 38671
www.endtimenephilim.com

ISBN: 978-0-9886814-1-5

## DEDICATION

To those who will read and come to know the truth that will set them free.

# Table of Contents

Introduction

Chapter 1
Time is Short! .................................................. 17

Chapter 2
Back to the Beginning ..................................... 19

Chapter 3
God's Heart for Man ....................................... 23

Chapter 4
An Angel Problem ........................................... 27

Chapter 5
Double Trouble for Earth ................................ 41

Chapter 6
The Fall ............................................................ 47

Chapter 7
Spirit Nature ................................................... 61

Chapter 8
Laws of Order .................................................. 65

Chapter 9
Cain and Able .................................................. 69

Chapter 10
Corruption of the Seed ................................... 77

Chapter 11
Nephilim .......................................................... 79

Chapter 12
Where on Earth?......................................................91

Chapter 13
Revealed in Ancient Hebrew ...................................93

Chapter 14
Defining to Expose................................................. 101

Chapter 15
Deviation ............................................................... 109

Chapter 16
Corrupt Seed ......................................................... 111

Chapter 17
Blending In............................................................ 115

Chapter 18
Tools for their Seed............................................... 117

Chapter 19
Access to the Body ................................................ 123

Chapter 20
Different Races of Giants ..................................... 129

Chapter 21
God's Responds..................................................... 131

Chapter 22
Sin and Unclean Spirits ....................................... 135

Chapter 23
Back to Noah ........................................................ 153

Chapter 24
Judgment............................................................... 163

Chapter 25
Mighty Men .................................................................. 169

Chapter 26
Mingled Seed ............................................................... 173

Chapter 27
Neanderthals and the Nephilim............................ 177

Chapter 28
Mindsets ....................................................................... 189

Chapter 29
Corruption of God's People .................................... 195

Chapter 30
Nephilim Webb........................................................... 203

Chapter 31
Covenant ...................................................................... 207

Chapter 32
Preparation of the Bride.......................................... 215

Chapter 33
Bride of Deceit –Fakes in our Midst..................... 217

Chapter 34
Sifting............................................................................ 231

Chapter 35
Faith Upholds the Commandments ..................... 237

Chapter 36
Enemy of Righteousness ......................................... 227

Chapter 37
Sealing........................................................................... 243

Chapter 38
Signs of the End of this Age ................................... 247

Chapter 39
The Bride Must Be Ready! ...................................... 253

Chapter 40
Come Out from Among Them ............................... 257

Chapter 41
Tree of Life, Tree of Good and Evil ........................ 261

Conclusion ............................................................. 264

A Warning from Heaven ......................................... 265

Source Notes .......................................................... 269

Sources .................................................................. 282

# Foreword

## My Wife the Author

Over ten years ago my wife Vickie began a new journey into the Scriptures; I would say she was looking for truth. Instinctively, deep inside something was amiss, just beyond her understanding. The Lord had something for her to grasp and to share that would change lives forever.

I watched her spend the vast majority of every single day for the last ten years pouring over scriptures in many translations. She read ancient texts, studied ancient languages, and read university studies. I have felt for her as she agonized making sure everything she wrote was in line with God's Word. The one thing stood out to me over the decade of her research and writing of this book. She has labored over every word and every line to make sure it is what God has truly said in his Word. In over 25 years of marriage, I have come to know Vickie as the most tenacious student of the Word of God that I have ever met.

# Introduction

## What Is Going On?

I found myself a passenger in a black, Lincoln Continental on an excursion in an unfamiliar place. My Christian guides appeared to be identical, with bright, shiny faces. One was a driver and another sat at my back. I looked ahead, and my eyes locked onto a scowl, drawn face as my driver announced, "He is a Nephilim." A blond haired giant of a man stood on a housetop in a tightly knit neighborhood so typical among us. His neatly pressed jeans and lumber-jack shirt was a common sight for this time of year. As we drove by, a pretense of work did not hinder his fixed gaze locked upon us. My second guide chimed in, "Oh yes, he's a Nephilim." My thoughts as they spoke, *How could it be, the Nephilim were no more.*

Next, I could see inside his apricot bricked home as my eyes panned a dimly lit overview which displayed as clean and tidy. With my view moving down a hall into a laundry room, my attention fixed on a window above and to the right of a washer and dryer. The sunlight waned as it filtered through the glass panes at late afternoon; the darkness of night would soon fall. Oddly, no other source of light could be seen anywhere in his house. Dreaming, I suddenly awoke. The Nephilim? What has that got to do with anything?" I thought.

This dream came at a time when a series of events unleashed hell into our midst which became unbearable. An unraveling maze of deception remained of what had been a lie. Now it seemed the Lord wanted my attention on the Nephilim. I could remember reading about them in the Old Testament, but nothing more.

Not long after waking, the title of this book dropped into my spirit. I knew I must study. *Living with the Nephilim, the Seed of Destruction* came as a result of that dream and years of research. I embarked on this journey with little knowledge and a lot of doubt, but with the help of the Holy Spirit, I transitioned to understand the Nephilim must be understood in this day and hour.

> My people are destroyed for lack of knowledge. Hosea 4:6 KJ

# Chapter 1

## Time is Short!

> As it was in the days of Noah, so it will be at the coming of the Son of Man.
> Matthew 24:37 NIV

We see and hear reports of war with rumors of more as violence, murder and mass slaying of innocence people fill the news. Even with this, the rise of evil has yet to reach its peak. What about the lonely that fall to seduction, only to find themselves lonely once again, left behind to debt, emotional wounds, and a youngster to raise alone? How about the missing loved one never to be heard from again, or those sexually abused by one so close to them. Let's not forget those society would like to trust, like politicians, sports directors, clergy, or anyone else about our everyday lives. All over the world pain and suffering must be endured at the hands of those with an appetite for more. Their appearance may not ring an alarm, but beneath the surface, another dimension rules these evil ones.

In my dream, the sun would shine only a few more hours, then darkness of night would fall. Interestingly from Genesis Chapter 1 a new day begins in the evening, at sundown. Of importance, the remaining light filtered over a place of cleansing and restoration.

Soiled garments must be washed before use. Clothing's first provision came from God after Adam and Eve sinned. The blood of an innocent animal covered their sin and its hide their bodies. The sunlight filtered from the right, and to the right His sheep are gathered.

> And he shall set the sheep on his right hand, but the goats on the left. Matthew 25:33 KLV

The day is almost over. God wants us to know, "A new day is coming; but there is time to be cleansed by the blood of the Lamb of God." Pressed upon my spirit, I knew to pen a warning for those who would listen: time is running out.

The Nephilim will not someday be in our mist; headline news confirms their presence. We must be armed with knowledge to recognize Nephilim in our everyday lives. In this book I go back to Creation and work forward to ensure a sound foundation of truth from the Word of God. Read a little, put it down, but pick it up again and finish to be prepared for what lies ahead.

# Chapter 2

# Back to the Beginning

> By faith we understand that the universe was formed at God's command, so that what is seen was not made out of what was visible. Hebrews 11:3

Humans touch two realms, the physical and spiritual, with a natural interaction with both. Our eyes function to give us sight in the physical world but do not see the super- natural reality about us. None-the-less, the unseen world exists. How do we know? Because the written Word of God gives us His testimony; our invisible God (a Spirit) spoke the physical world into existence. As humans we connect with the natural world through our five senses and must rely on God's written Word (Holy Bible) to gain knowledge about the spirit world we cannot see. Both dimensions (physical and spirit realms) interact and coexist at the same time. We cannot see the wind but experience the effects of a strong gust or a gentle breeze. The spirit realm functions in a similar way with the physical world. *To understand the Nephilim, we must also grasp how the spirit realm affects our physical world on an ongoing basis.*

> 20 For since the creation of the world God's invisible qualities—his eternal power and divine nature—have been clearly seen, being understood from what has been made, so that people are without excuse. Romans 1:20

Moses wrote the first five books of the Bible, or Pentateuch, leaving an account of God's dealings with mankind. In order to discern the Nephilim, we will go back to creation and work forward to understand how we got here.

> 1In the beginning God created the heavens and the earth. 2Now the earth was formless and empty, darkness was over the surface of the deep, and the Spirit of God was hovering over the waters. God said, "Let there be light," and there was light. 4 God saw that the light was good, and He separated the light from the darkness.5 God called the light "day," and the darkness he called "night." And there was evening, and there was morning—the first day.

God created everything needed for life on earth, which included living creatures and then man.

> 26 Then God said, "Let us make man in our image, in our likeness, and let them rule over the fish of the sea and the birds of the air, over the livestock, over all the earth, and over all the creatures that move along the ground." 27So God created man in his own image, in the image of God he created him; male and female he

> created them. 28 God blessed them and said to them, "Be fruitful and increase in number; fill the earth and subdue it. Rule over the fish of the sea and the birds of the air and over every living creature that moves on the ground." . . . 31 God saw all that he had made, and it was very good. And there was evening, and there was morning—the sixth day.

Formless, empty, and in darkness describe the "now" condition of earth in verse 2 of Genesis Chapter 1. The Spirit of God hovered and waited for the Word of God's release to bring order into chaos. "God said" and it came into existence with one exception (Genesis 1:3-31).

> 7 The Lord God formed the man from the dust of the ground and breathed into his nostrils the breath of life, and the man became a living being. Genesis 1:1-5, 26-28, 31; 2:7

God formed Adam from the dust of the ground and breathed breath of life into his nostrils (Genesis 2:7). "Formed," in Hebrew *yatsar,* means through the squeezing into shape.[1] *Man's creation came about by the hand of God, a significant point to remember when understanding the Nephilim.* God saw all he made including man and declared it very good!

> May your whole spirit, soul and body be kept blameless at the coming of our Lord Jesus Christ. 1Thessalonians 5:23b

As One Triune God, He consists as the Father, Son and Holy Spirit. Triune as well, each human consists of a spirit, with a soul that dwells in a physical body.

God established man's world and gave him commands to ensure success and authority to rule it. For example, Adam made the decision on names for each living creature, and whatever Adam decided became their names (Genesis 2:19).

> 28 God blessed them and said to them, "Be fruitful and increase in number; fill the earth and subdue it. Rule over the fish of the sea and the birds of the air and over every living creature that moves on the ground." Genesis 1:28

# Chapter 3

## God's Heart for Man

8And the LORD God planted a garden eastward in Eden; and there he put the man whom he had formed. 9And out of the ground made the LORD God to grow every tree that is pleasant to the sight, and good for food; the tree of life also in the midst of the garden, and the tree of knowledge of good and evil. 15And the LORD God took the man, and put him into the garden of Eden to dress it and to keep it.16And the LORD God commanded the man, saying, Of every tree of the garden thou mayest freely eat: 17But of the tree of the knowledge of good and evil, thou shalt not eat of it: for in the day that thou eatest thereof thou shalt surely die. Genesis 2:8-9; 15-17 KJ

Life surely thrived for both Adam and Eve. They enjoyed peace and surroundings of splendor with God's presence in an ongoing relationship of spiritual unity. Adam and Eve's garden home consisted of not just one tree, but every tree pleasing to the eyes and good for food. God's provision for man consisted of a place to call home, food in ample supply, beautiful surroundings, work for his hands, and a wife to make a family. In this pre-sin state, God's glory manifest in all their lives signifying his goodness and intent for mankind's existence on earth. God demonstrated his call to the individual by forming one Adam and giving him full liberty to live and accomplish his tasks according to the guidelines God set. When God brought Eve from Adam's side, God continued to relate not only with the individual but to them both.

> Now the LORD God had formed out of the ground all the beasts of the field and all the birds of the air. He brought them to the man to see what he would name them; and whatever the man called each living creature, that was its name. Genesis 2:19

"And they heard the voice of the LORD God walking in the garden in the cool of the day: and Adam and his wife hid themselves from the presence of the LORD God amongst the trees of the garden (Genesis 3:8 KJ)." The word for garden in Genesis 2:15, *ganan*, means a garden enclosure, like a fence. Interestingly, the garden God planted in Eden happened to be a defensive structure for Adam and Eve. The root word for garden is ganan, to defend, cover, and surround. It was always used to show God's protection as a covering.[2]

Opportunity to eat fruit from the vast variety in the garden sounds pretty good, but Adam and Eve must not eat from one particular tree, "the tree of the knowledge of good and evil." Two trees in the middle of the garden symbolized two different choices for the people on earth.

One tree brought forth fruit of an ongoing life in union with God; the second tree's fruit produced separation from God and death. The tree of life stood to remind Adam and Eve of the life they enjoyed, given and sustained by God. In a state of obedience, they could partake of any fruit in the garden, but one, including the tree of life at this point. The forbidden fruit, the only "could not" command given them by God, would prove fatal if ignored. Adam and Eve must be tested. God revealed himself. They must know His ways, spoken and demonstrated, to pass the test. In the New Testament Jesus spoke, "If anyone loves God, they will obey His command." (John 14:15) Did they love him? God gave mankind freedom to make this choice.

> If you love me, you will obey what I command. John 14:15

Along with the structure of the garden and a direct command to avoid death, "Don't eat that fruit!" (Genesis 2:17) Adam's job to tend, guard, and keep the garden should have kept him vigilant. 15And the Lord God took the man and put him in the Garden of Eden to tend and guard and keep it. Genesis 2:15 Amplified Bible

A guard also describes one of Eve's job descriptions in aide to her husband. As his wife, Eve worked with Adam in what God called them together to accomplish. Eve, as well as Adam, played a part in guarding, tending, and keeping the garden.

> The LORD God said, "It is not good for the man to be alone. I will make a helper suitable for him." Genesis 2:18

God's protection was clear. Adam did not need to fall. All he needed to do was keep God's command. We may criticize Adam and Eve or even be angry at their failure in the garden, but a closer look will help us understand just what they were up against.

> 20My son, pay attention to what I say, listen closely to my words.21 Do not let them out of your sight, keep them within your heart; 22 for they are life to those who find them and health to a man's whole body. 23Above all else, guard your heart, for it is the wellspring of life. Proverbs 4:20-23

# Chapter 4

# An Angel Problem

> 14 I will ascend above the heights of the clouds; I will make myself like the Most High. Isaiah 14:14 Amplified Bible

Why would God put Adam and Eve in a garden with the tree of life and knowledge of good and evil? I believe God created the first heaven and earth with the second heaven and earth in mind. Why? God had an angel problem.

> 13But in keeping with his promise we are looking forward to a new heaven and a new earth, the home of righteousness. 2 Peter 3:13

Remember, Genesis 1:31a, "God saw all that he had made, and it was very good." Angels, created by God, came under this declaration.

> Thus the heavens and the earth were finished, and all the host of them. Genesis 2:1

Angels as well as mankind are spoken of in scripture as "God's elect." Elect angels serve God as He originally in- tended and continue to do even now.

> I charge you, in the sight of God and Christ Jesus and the elect angels, to keep these instructions without partiality, and to do nothing out of favoritism. 1Timothy 5:17

> And he will send his angels and gather his elect from the four winds, from the ends of the earth to the ends of the heavens. Mark 13:27

God created different types of angels in various ranks and positions of authority (Ephesians 6:12): arch angels, cherubim, seraphim, and watcher or guardian angels.

> Above him were seraphs, each with six wings: With two wings they covered their faces, with two they covered their feet, and with two they were flying. Isaiah 6: 2

> "This sentence is by the decree of the angelic watchers and the decision is a command of the holy ones. . . Daniel 4:17a NASB

> Then Michael, one of the archangels, came to help me, and I left him there with the spirit prince of the kingdom of Persia. Daniel 10:13b NLT

Not all angels remain as God's elect; not all men are God's elect either. When once holy angels sinned, they became fallen angels, rejected by God. "Then he will say to those on his left, 'Depart from me, you who are cursed, into the eternal fire prepared for *the devil and his angels*. Matthew 25:41

This angel problem began with one angel, an anointed cherub, called Lucifer. As a class of angel, cherubim over-shadow God's throne in heaven (Ezekiel 28:14) and stretched over the Ark of the Covenant in the Tent of Meeting (Exodus, chapters 25-27).

> "O LORD Almighty, God of Israel, enthroned between the cherubim, you alone are God over all the kingdoms of the earth. You have made heaven and earth. Isaiah 37:16

Cherubim also happen to be the type of angel sent to remove Adam and Eve from the Garden of Eden, keeping them from the tree of life. (Genesis 3:24).

> 24 After he drove the man out, he placed on the east side of the Garden of Eden cherubim and a flaming sword flashing back and forth to guard the way to the tree of life. Genesis 3:24

Oh how God fashioned this guardian cherubim, a spectacular sight: radiating beams of light, sparkling in glorious color from every precious stone set in gold (Ezekiel 28:13). Filled, then sealed with the sum of God given wisdom and beauty, it seems God found no problem with this cherub until iniquity came forth from the depth of his own heart. "11Moreover the word of the LORD came unto me, saying, 12 Son of man, take up a lamentation upon the king of Tyrus, and say unto him, Thus saith the Lord

GOD; Thou sealest up the sum, full of wisdom, and perfect in beauty. 13Thou hast been in Eden the garden of God; every precious stone was thy covering, the sardius, topaz, and the diamond, the beryl, the onyx, and the jasper, the sapphire, the emerald, and the carbuncle, and gold: the workmanship of thy tabrets and of thy pipes was prepared in thee in the day that thou wast created. 14Thou art the anointed cherub that covereth; and I have set thee so: thou wast upon the holy mountain of God; thou hast walked up and down in the midst of the stones of fire.15Thou wast perfect in thy ways from the day that thou wast created, till iniquity was found in thee. 16By the multitude of thy merchandise they have filled the midst of thee with **violence**, and thou hast sinned: therefore I will cast thee as profane out of the mountain of God: and I will destroy thee, O covering cherub, from the midst of the stones of fire.17Thine heart was lifted up because of thy beauty, thou hast **corrupted** thy wisdom by reason of thy brightness: I will cast thee to the ground, I will lay thee before kings, that they may behold thee. " Ezekiel 28:11-17 KJ

In Ezekiel 28:1 we see the spirit and physical realm at work as the "ruler" of Tyrus speaks of a man, but the "king" of Tyrus is a diabolical spirit who operates through the human ruler of Tyrus. "King" (Ezekiel 28:12) in Hebrew "melek", refers to a royal and can be translated as Moloch (known by various names), a false god of the Canaanites and Phoenicians.[3] Here we see "king" used for a fallen spirit who exalted himself to be worshiped as a god, greatly influencing a human ruler of the nation of Tyrus.

> "1The word of the LORD came again unto me, saying, 2"Son of man, say to the ruler of Tyre, this is what the Sovereign LORD says, "In the pride of your heart you say, "I am a god; I sit on the throne of a god in the heart of the seas." But you are a man and not a god, though you think you are as wise as a god." Ezekiel 28:1-2

The prophet Ezekiel, speaking by the word of the Lord concerning the King of Tyrus, revealed this fallen cherub who had been in Eden, the garden of God. Take notice of two words "corrupt" and "violence" ascribed to Lucifer; we will see how these words relate to the Nephilim as we go along. Isaiah, another prophet of God also received revelation from the Lord concerning this angel.

> 12 "How you have fallen from heaven, O star of the morning, son of the dawn! You have been cut down to the earth, You who have weakened the nations!13 "But you said in your heart, 'I will ascend to heaven; I will raise my throne above the stars of God, And I will sit on the mount of assembly In the recesses of the north. Isaiah 14:12-14 NASB

Out of the essence of Lucifer's being, his abominable "I wills" erupt. "You said in your heart, 'I will ascend to heaven; I will raise my throne above the stars of God; I will sit enthroned on the mount of assembly, on the utmost heights of the sacred mountain. I will ascend above the tops of the clouds; I will make myself like the Most High'."(Isaiah 14:13-14) Lucifer conceived steps of action to achieve his ultimate goal, ascension to the utmost heights, to the very top, "I will be like God

(Isaiah 14:14)." Satan's rebellion began with pride, then a lie, (belief he was a god). Next came deception, and then action to make it happen. At this point, sin existed in Lucifer alone and none other. Enthroned as god in his own heart, no longer would Lucifer glorify his Creator and God. As iniquities conception becomes clearly exposed, he disregards Jehovah's sovereignty and set up a separate kingdom, right here. Once he declared, "I will," God had a defiant, determined angel, who intended to dominate and do whatever he pleased to secure his own exaltation, to be "like the Most High" (Isaiah 14:14). Lucifer wanted his will, his way, and dictated to God what he would do. He became the first dictator and rebellion's architect who came out of harmony with God's order and stepped into unauthorized territory. Satan became God's mimicker and clearly a self-deceived counterfeit to believe he could take God's place. Lifting of another in God's stead displaces the Most High from his rightful position, as Lord of lords and King of kings. God cannot tolerate rebellion and unrighteousness, for He is Holy. Instead of giving God worship, Lucifer would demand it for himself, thus replacing truth of God for a lie, birthing worship of self, idolatry, lust, immorality, false religion, and the list goes on.

> By the multitude of thy merchandise they have filled the midst of thee with violence, and thou hast sinned: Ezekiel 28:16a

The Hebrew word for violence, "chamac," in Ezekiel 28:16, means "cruelty, oppression and wrong with its root word meaning, to treat or oppress violently and injure both ethically and physically." [4] With the use of a thesaurus and synonyms, we gain more insight of the depth and magnitude of evil one angel birthed.

Cruelty- defined as deliberate infliction of pain and suffering, [5] "violence, murder, brutality, bestiality, abusive, cold-heartedness, inhumane, atrocity, sadism, savagery, barbaric, ruthlessness, animality and devilry."[6]

"Oppression- defined as the act of subjugating by cruelty.[7] [8] "Brutality, coercion, conquering, control, cruelty, despotism, dictatorship, domination, fascism, force, injustice, maltreatment, martial law, overthrowing, persecution, subduing, subjection, suffering, terrorism, torment and tyranny." [9]

"Wrong- defined as contrary to conscience or morality or law." [10] Wicked, deplorable, reprehensible, unethical, crime, cruelty, genocide, evil, harm, immoral, vicious, imposition, indecency, depraved, inhumane, inequity, injustice, malevolence, oppression, persecution, prejudice, untrue, slander, transgression, unjust, vice, wicked, sin." [11]

In Ezekiel 28, the nation of Tyre traded among many nations and became a world leader in commerce through its merchant ships. But something else stands out as I read Ezekiel 28:16a, "By the multitude of thy merchandise they have filled the midst of thee with violence, and thou hast sinned." The Amplified Bible states this a little differently, "Through the abundance of your commerce you were filled with lawlessness and violence, and you sinned." Adding words from Ezekiel 28:18a, "Many sins and dishonest trade," reveals a greedy and oppressive nation whose lawlessness brought abundant riches.

> For the love of money is the root of all evil: which while some coveted after, they have erred from the faith, and pierced themselves through with many sorrows. I Timothy 6:10 KJ

The ruler of Tyrus (a man) full of pride, believing he was a god, epitomizes this pompous, fallen angel, clearly displaying his essence.

> Thine heart was lifted up because of thy beauty; *thou hast corrupted thy wisdom by reason of thy brightness: Ezekiel 28:17*

Corruption ruins original intent for someone or something's planned use. *Shachath,* the Hebrew word for corrupted in Ezekiel 28:17 means" to corrupt, destroy, go to ruin, decay."[12] God originally set Lucifer as a cherub that covered, but he unset himself by sin and forever destroyed his holiness and ability to cover as a righteous cherub. Lucifer's worship shifted from God to himself which set him on a course to deflect worship away from God. Being perverse, any worship that he promoted would be false.

To be as god, Lucifer must be exalted and worshipped. He also needed help, but unable to create a new, he sought angels for his service. Lies and falsehood will be found at the root of deception, so to be tempted by the devil, angels first needed to entertain his lies. What is deception? "As defined it is the act of misleading, false representation or fraud."[13] Lucifer would mislead fellow angels using the same process by which he fell. First, a lie spoken or portrayed or maybe a combination of both, a thought pondered to the point of desire, then lust acted upon which ends in sin.

So deception's lie conceived in the heart, replayed in the mind by thoughts, there either rejected or accepted. If accepted and acted upon, sin is birthed. He became a counterfeit of the one true God by simply portraying him.

While seducing fellow angels and disarming them by his charm, Lucifer went about setting up his own kingdom. He became more and more driven to dominate as violence erupted from the depth of his being. Lucifer wanted what he wanted and cast off all restraint to get it, as a complete transformation to wickedness occurred. Satan acted on what he purposed in his heart to accomplish and ensnared a third of all angels who also rebelled against God. With their help, Satan sought control of heaven and initiated war (a first brought on by the devil). Arch angel Michael fought against the dragon and his angels. The dragon and his angels, not as strong, were hurled from heaven to earth. Kicked out of heaven, where could Lucifer set up his throne? Earth, but God gave it to man. No problem. He would steal it from man and rework earth to glorify him. Satan wanted humans to take on his debased nature so he could be their god. Any influence of righteousness as established by God must be deluded, confused, and destroyed. This war between good and evil fell to earth.

> 3Then another sign appeared in heaven: an enormous red dragon with seven heads and ten horns and seven crowns on his heads. 4His tail swept a third of the stars out of the sky and flung them to the earth. There was war in heaven. Michael and his angels fought against the dragon, and the dragon and his angels fought back. 8But he was not strong enough, and

> they lost their place in heaven. 9The great dragon was hurled down--that ancient serpent called the devil, or Satan, who leads the whole world astray. He was hurled to the earth, and his angels with him. Revelations 12:3, 7-9

> Behold, he put no trust in his servants; and his angels he charged with folly: Job 4:18 KJ

A Biblical example of how deception works to take over a kingdom would be the story of Absalom. Absalom, a son of King David, went routinely to the city gates to gain a loyal following. Exalting himself above King David, he stole the people's heart in an attempt to take the throne from his father, using deception to achieve his goal.

Absalom exalted himself as king, while submitted and faithful followers of King David rose up to protect him and his throne. A battle ensued, and Absalom was destroyed. What sin do we see concerning Absalom? Absalom, a man greatly praised because of his handsome appearance, be- came self-exalted and proud, which led him to be deceived so that he should attain the throne. Sounds much like the scenario of Lucifer in heaven (2 Samuel 18:14-18).

> 18During his lifetime Absalom had taken a pillar and erected it in the King's Valley as a monument to himself, for he thought, "I have no son to carry on the memory of my name." He named the pillar after himself, and it is called Absalom's Monument to this day. 2 Samuel18:18

25In all Israel there was not a man so highly praised for his handsome appearance as Absalom. From the top of his head to the sole of his foot there was no blemish in him. 26Whenever he cut the hair of his head—he used to cut his hair from time to time when it became too heavy for him—he would weigh it, and its weight was two hundred shekels by the royal standard. 2 Samuel 14:25-26

1In the course of time, Absalom provided himself with a chariot and horses and with fifty men to run ahead of him. 2He would get up early and stand by the side of the road leading to the city gate. Whenever anyone came with a complaint to be placed before the king for a decision, Absalom would call out to him, "What town are you from?" He would answer, "Your servant is from one of the tribes of Israel." 3Then Absalom would say to him, "Look, your claims are valid and proper, but there is no representative of the king to hear you." 4And Absalom would add, "If only I were appointed judge in the land! Then everyone who has a complaint or case could come to me and I would see that he gets justice." 5 Also, whenever anyone approached him to bow down before him, Absalom would reach out his hand,take hold of him and kiss him. 6Absalom behaved in this way toward all the Israelites who came to the king asking for justice, and so he stole the hearts of the men of Israel. 7At the end of four years, Absalom said to the king, "Let me go to Hebron and fulfill a vow I made to the Lord. 8While your servant was living at Geshur in Aram, I made this vow: 'If the Lord takes me back to Jerusalem, I will worship the Lord in Hebron.'" 9The king said to him, "Go in peace." So he went to Hebron.

10Then Absalom sent secret messengers throughout the tribes of Israel to say, "As soon as you hear the sound of the trumpets, then say, 'Absalom is king in Hebron.'" 11Two hundred men from Jerusalem had accompanied Absalom. They had been invited as guests and went quite innocently, knowing nothing about the matter. 12While Absalom was offering sacrifices, he also sent for Ahithophel the Gilonite, David's counselor, to come from Giloh, his hometown. And so the conspiracy gained strength, and Absalom's following kept on increasing. 2 Samuel 15:1-12

Easton's Bible Dictionary provides a good overview of this fallen angel, Satan.

> "Adversary or accuser when used as a proper name, the Hebrew word so rendered has the article 'the adversary'" (Job 1:6-12; 2:1-7). In the New Testament it is used as interchangeable with the devil and is so used more than thirty times. He is also called "the dragon," "the old serpent" (Rev. 12:9; 20:2), "the prince of this world" (John 12:31; 14:30), "the prince of the power of the air" (Eph. 2:2), "the god of this world" (2 Cor. 4:4), and "the spirit that now works in the children of disobedience" (Eph. 2:2). The distinct personality of Satan and his activity among men are thus obviously recognized. He tempted our Lord in the wilderness (Matt. 4:1-11). He is "Beelzebub, the prince of the devils" 12:24). He is "the constant enemy of God, of Christ, of the divine kingdom, of the followers of Christ, and of all truth; full of falsehood and all

malice, and exciting and seducing to evil in every possible way." His power is very great in the world. He is a "roaring lion, seeking whom he may devour" (1 Pet. 5:8). Men are said to be "taken captive by him" (2 Tim. 2:26). Christians are warned against his "devices" (2 Cor. 2:11) and called to "resist" him (James 4:7). Christ redeems his people from "him that had the power of death, that is, the devil" (Heb. 2:14).14

In his book *Hebrew Word Pictures: How Does the Hebrew Alphabet Reveal Prophetic Truths*, Dr. Frank T. Seekins defined Satan as "the snake that devours life."15 Hebrew Word Pictures uses each letter of an ancient Hebrew word to add a "pictorial understanding" and this picture is clear, Satan destroys life.

Satan's master plan was to fill earth with people just like him. With his own seed he would control earth and reign as god. His seed oppose righteousness, live by their sin nature, and have nothing much in the area of human conscious. Just like Satan, they set out to destroy any goodness in life as established by God. Satan would produce his version of mankind in his image and nature. It does not matter what country, race, what field of activity, whether young or old, his seed dwells among us.

Satan and his angels will intensify their activities as it gets closer to the return of the Lord. Satan failed in heaven and will meet his end, but until the time when the Son of God comes to destroy his kingdom, we must understand we also have an angel problem.

# Chapter 5

## Double Trouble for Earth

> They serve at a sanctuary that is a copy and shadow of what is in heaven. This is why Moses was warned when he was about to build the tabernacle: "See to it that you make everything according to the pattern shown you on the mountain." Hebrews 8:5

A closer study of cherubim unfolds additional information we need to consider. Moses received directions to build a tabernacle modeled exactly as specified by God. He was warned not to deviate from this pattern as it replicated the tabernacle in heaven (Exodus 25). With wings stretched upward, two golden cherubim overshadowed the atonement cover in the Holy of Holies, above the ark of the Testimony.

> 17"Make an atonement cover of pure gold—two and a half cubits long and a cubit and a half wide. 18And make two cherubim out of hammered gold at the ends of the cover. 19Make one cherub on one end and the second cherub on the other; make the cherubim of one piece with the cover, at the two ends. 20The cherubim are to have their wings spread upward, overshadowing the cover with them. The

cherubim are to face each other, looking toward the cover. 21Place the cover on top of the ark and put in the ark the Testimony, which I will give you. 22There, above the cover between the two cherubim that are over the ark of the Testimony, I will meet with you and give you all my commands for the Israelites. Exodus 25:17-22 NIV

Solomon followed this same pattern as well in the temple he built for the Lord (I Kings 6, 2 Chronicles 3).

23In the inner sanctuary he made a pair of cherubim of olive wood, each ten cubits high. 24One wing of the first cherub was five cubits long, and the other wing five cubits—ten cubits from wing tip to wing tip. 25The second cherub also measured ten cubits, **for the two cherubim were identical in size and shape.** 26The height of each cherub was ten cubits. 27He placed the cherubim inside the innermost room of the temple, with their wings spread out. The wing of one cherub touched one wall, while the wing of the other touched the other wall, and their wings touched each other in the middle of the room. 28He overlaid the cherubim with gold. 1 Kings 6:23-28 NIV

As their wings touched, the pair of angels overshadowed the mercy seat of the Ark of the Covenant. In the ark was the stone tablet of the covenant, Aaron's budded staff, and a jar of manna, all supernatural signs of God's power and covenant of mercy.

> 3Behind the second curtain was a room called the Most Holy Place, 4which had the golden altar of incense and the gold-covered Ark of the Covenant. This ark contained the gold jar of manna, Aaron's staff that had budded, and the stone tablets of the covenant. 5Above the ark were the cherubim of the Glory, overshadowing the atonement cover. Hebrews 9:1-5 NIV

In other scriptural accounts of cherub angels, Ezekiel saw four cherubim at one time (Ezekiel 1:5). King David described God's determination to save him as he rode a single cherub to his rescue (Psalms 18:10). But as a duplicate of the heavenly tabernacle, two cherubim were required in the Holy of Holies.

> 20The cherubim are to have their wings spread upward, overshadowing the cover with them. The cherubim are to face each other, looking toward the cover. Exodus 25:20 NIV

These two cherubim were created "as one" with the cover of the mercy seat, overshadowed "as one" with touched wings, and functioned "as one" in service to God. As each angel faced one another, they looked toward the cover of the mercy seat. These as, "existing, acting, or considered as a single unit, entity, or individual." specifications indicates unity and harmony as a part of their creation and call as cherubim. Think about the oneness of these two angels with "one" in this context "You were the anointed cherub who covers, And I placed you there. You were on the holy mountain of God; You walked in the midst of the stones of fire. Ezekiel 28:14 NASB

Notice Ezekiel 28:14 was written in past tense. Lucifer was placed as the anointed cherub who covers, located in heaven on the mountain of God. Lucifer was ordained as one part of this pair of cherubim. I believe the other half of this pair was Abaddon.

As cherubim, their names provide revelation about them. Originally, these two angels emanated God's glory of light and life. Lucifer was the cherub of light, and Abaddon the cherub of life, but in a fallen state, they became an entity of darkness and death.[17] Abaddon in Hebrew means destruction, and Apollyon in Greek means destroyer.

> . . . a king over them the angel of the Abyss, whose name in Hebrew is Abaddon, and in Greek, Apollyon. Rev 9: 11b

Abaddon is the angelic prince of the infernal regions, the minister of death, and the author of havoc on the earth.[18] Lucifer is the angel of darkness but appears as an angel of light in order to deceive (1 Corinthians 11:14).[19]

> To give light to them that sit in darkness and [in] the shadow of death, to guide our feet into the way of peace. Luke 1:79 KJ

"Darkness" in Luke 1:79 is the word skotos in Greek, "as a figure of speech it means; those who are in moral or spiritual darkness," along with the root word skia, that is "the image" or "outline" cast by an object, a shadow."20 Now putting these words together as covering cherubim, their image once cast light and life, but as apostates, these angels cast the shadow of darkness and death. With this study, an angelic affect can be understood; they cast a shadow illuminating their essence. As angels move about, their presence can be detected by the type of shadow they cast or the effect of their presence upon those in their shadow.

Those in darkness are under the shadow of death, which is the effect of these two fallen angels (Luke 1:79). The shadow of death falls over land and people (Matthew 4:16).

The people walking in darkness have seen a great light; on those living in the land of the shadow of death a light has dawned. Isaiah 9:2

King David in Psalm 143:3 was under an oppression of darkness which weighed down his soul.

The enemy pursues me, he crushes me to the ground; he makes me dwell in darkness like those long dead.[4] so my spirit grows faint within me; my heart within me is dismayed. Psalm 143:3 4

This was the effect of darkness and death that overshadowed him from the spirit realm. Notice his spirit grew weak, and he became discouraged. These words were spoken by "a man after God's own heart" (Acts 13:22) If such heaviness came over King David, think about the rest of man- kind. Another fact about these two cherubim, they were identical in size and shape (1 Kings 6:25). Identical as defined "The same; the selfsame; the very same; not different."[21] Lucifer and Abaddon are two different angels, but dead ringers one for the other. Not a problem in service to God but a major problem as apostates. As Lucifer's angelic partner, Abaddon came in agreement with Lucifer's rebel- lion. The focus of their gaze had been on God's mercy but no longer. Mercy far removed, their shadow transports dark- ness and death to keep men from the merciful atonement provided by God through Jesus Christ.

# Chapter 6

# The Fall

> It is written, Man shall not live by bread alone, but by every word that proceedeth out of the mouth of God. Matthew 4:4 KJ

Formed as adults, Adam and Eve did not experience childhood as those born from human parents (Genesis 2:7-22). Clad in innocence, God's essence of love nurtured and prepared them for life on earth. Adam and Eve related to the Spirit of God in a bond of trust, unity and peace, until one day it all changed.

> God is love; and he that dwelleth in love dwelleth in God, and God in him. 1 John 4:16b KJ

Observed by the deceiver, he too wanted to relate with Adam and Eve but certainly not out of love. Satan would work from the supernatural realm to invade the natural world in which man lived. As a spirit, he sought use of a physical form to gain the couple's trust, and since Adam named each living creature, none would be any better than a serpent (Genesis 2:19).

1 Now the serpent was more crafty than any wild animal which Adonai God, had made. He said to the woman, "Did God really say, "You are not to eat from any tree in the garden?" 2The woman answered the serpent, "We may eat from the fruit of the trees of the garden, 3 but about the fruit of the tree in the middle of the garden God said, "You are neither to eat from it nor touch it, or you will die." 4 The serpent said to the woman: It is not true that you will surely die: 5 because God knows that on the day you eat from it, your eyes will be opened, and you will be like God, knowing good and evil: 6 When the woman saw that the tree was good for food that it had a pleasing appearance and that the tree was desirable for making one wise, she took some of its fruit and ate. She also gave some to her husband, who was with her; and he ate 7 Then the eyes of both of them were opened, and they realized that they were naked. So they sewed fig leaves together to make themselves loincloths. Genesis 3:1-7 Complete Jewish Bible

The serpent described as "crafty" which means, "skillful in evil more than any other wild animal of the field" seems odd to me (Genesis 3:1). I do not think in terms of wild animals possessing evil schemes at this point in earth's history, maybe a scheme to acquire food, but before the fall animals ate vegetation seemingly in amble supply.

> And to all the beasts of the earth and all the birds of the air and all the creatures that move on the ground—everything that has the breath of life in it—I give every green plant for food." And it was so. Genesis 1:30

Out of the supernatural realm, angelic interference seems already at work to disrupt God's structure on earth. We see this as true because Satan, a rebellious, angel, embodied the serpent in the garden, an uninvited invasion from the supernatural world into God's order on earth.

> He was hurled to the earth, and his angels with him. Revelations 12:9c NIV

To unfold this attack on Eve and Adam, a closer look at *nachash*, the Hebrew root word for serpent will benefit us. *Nachash* means to hiss or whisper, which also describes the sounds of a serpent. It denotes "the whisper of a soothsayer and to practice enchantment, divination or to use sorcery against."[22] Satan unleashed supernatural tools to divide Adam and Eve from God, a work underway much sooner than Genesis chapter three. Once achieved, the devil seized Adam's authority to rule on earth and placed mankind into bondage to sin.

> Then God said, "Let us make man in our image, in our likeness, and let them rule over the fish of the sea and the birds of the air, over the livestock, over all the earth, and over all the creatures that move along the ground. Genesis 1:26

Going to the dialog of Genesis chapter three, the serpents to Eve, "Did God really say (Genesis 3:1)?" This questions the truthfulness of Adam who initially heard the command from God, placing Eve in a position of doubting, then defending what God spoke originally to Adam. Eve appears all too comfortable conversing with a serpent and tells him, "We may eat from the fruit of the trees of the garden, but about the fruit of the tree in the middle of the garden God said, 'You are neither to eat from it nor touch it, or you will die'" (Genesis 3:3-4). In her call as Adam's wife, Eve allied with him to follow God's commands as given to Adam. Adam instructed her concerning these commands (Genesis 3:3), but God did not say "not to touch it, or you will die." Adam may have added "do not touch" to keep Eve away from the tree. "Not to touch" added to the original command, could indicate Adam did not fully trust Eve. Perhaps Eve's desirous talk for the forbidden fruit brought concern to Adam, so he added a "not to touch" requirement.

A dialogue between Adam and his wife may have gone like this: "Honey, you sure are spending a lot of time with the serpent lately." "Yes, Adam, he seems to be close by at all times," spoke, Eve. "He's so nice and pleasant. I get some of the weirdest thoughts when he is around though. Have you seen the trees in the midst of the garden, especially the beautiful fruit on the tree to know good and evil?" Adam spoke, "You know we cannot eat from that tree or we will die, so don't touch that tree!" "Oh, I won't," Eve spoke, as she ran along. Off in the distance, the serpent waited to join her as she went about her day.

When the woman saw that the fruit of the tree was good for food and pleasing to the eye, and also desirable for gaining wisdom, she took some and ate it. She also gave some to her husband, who was with her, and he ate it.

> 4"You will not surely die," the serpent said to the woman. 5 "For God knows that when you eat of it your eyes will be opened, and you will be like God, knowing good and evil." Genesis 3:4-6 NIV

Satan's slyness breaks down Eve's focus from the command of God, "to not eating," to standing right by the tree. "Oh, how absolutely wonderful and delicious the fruit on this tree must be. Surely we can eat it. We just misunderstood," she could have reasoned. Eve did not realize it, but thoughts such as these shift truth to a lie and attach a character of Satan onto God. Thoughts or just slight impressions as these would redirect their attention to themselves. A final blow to their obedience came in the delicious fruit of pride. "You'll be like God, if you eat this fruit" (Genesis 3:5). Such words were spoken to lure and motivate, finding satisfaction only by eating the forbidden fruit, possibly replaying in Eve's mind. A desire to be "like God" certainly originates from Satan, and the final straw to entrap the first couple. As they let go of God's word from their hearts, sin took over as they exalted themselves above God's command. Desire turned into lust of the flesh, lust of the eyes, and pride of life, only one step left: a bite of death. Adam stood by as the serpent enticed his wife, but through him the prize would be won.

> When tempted, no one should say, "God is tempting me." For God cannot be tempted by evil, nor does he tempt anyone; but each one is tempted when, by his own evil desire, he is dragged away and enticed. Then, after desire has conceived, it gives birth to sin; and sin, when it is full- grown, gives birth to death. James 1:13-15 NIV

Scripture reveals Adam did not fall into Satan's deception but disobeyed the command of God. Out of rebellion Adam ate the forbidden fruit, but Eve became ensnared by the trickery of the deceiver.

> And Adam was not the one deceived; it was the woman who was deceived and became a sinner. 1 Timothy 2:14 KJ

Adam and Eve ate their way and ours into a fallen, sinful state in taking on the spiritual nature of Satan. This entire process originates from the diabolical, spirit realm to change man's God-centered life to a self-centered life oblivious to Him. No longer covered by the glory of God, Adam and Eve entered spiritual earth as their naked bodies exposed their shame.

> 8 Then the man and his wife heard the sound of the LORD God as he was walking in the garden in the cool of the day, and they hid from the LORD God among the trees of the garden. 9 But the LORD God called to the man, "Where are you?" 10 He answered, "I heard you in the garden, and I was afraid because I was

naked; so I hid." 11 And he said, "Who told you that you were naked? Have you eaten from the tree that I commanded you not to eat from?" 12 The man said, "The woman you put here with me—she gave me some fruit from the tree, and I ate it." 13 Then the LORD God said to the woman, "What is this you have done?" The woman said, "The serpent deceived me, and I ate."14 So the Lord God said to the serpent, "Because you have done this, "Cursed are you above all the livestock and all the wild animals! You will crawl on your belly and you will eat dust all the days of your life. 15 And I will put enmity between you and the woman, and between your offspring and hers; he will crush your head, and you will strike his heel." 16 To the woman he said, "I will greatly increase your pains in childbearing; with pain you will give birth to children. Your desire will be for your husband, and he will rule over you." 17 To Adam he said, "Because you listened to your wife and ate from the tree about which I commanded you, 'You must not eat of it,' "Cursed is the ground because of you; through painful toil you will eat of it all the days of your life. 18 It will produce thorns and thistles for you, and you will eat the plants of the field. 19 By the sweat of your brow you will eat your food until you return to the ground, since from it you were taken; for dust you are and to dust you will return." 20 Adam named his wife Eve, because she would become the mother of all the living. 21 The Lord God made garments of skin for Adam and his wife and clothed them. 22 And the

> Lord God said, "The man has now become like one of us, knowing good and evil. He must not be allowed to reach out his hand and take also from the tree of life and eat, and live forever." 23 So the Lord God banished him from the Garden of Eden to work the ground from which he had been taken. 24After he drove the man out, he placed on the east side of the Garden of Eden cherubim and a flaming sword flashing back and forth to guard the way to the tree of life. Genesis 3:8-24 NIV

Under the blessing of God, the ground had produced what was good and pleasing for them. Due to Adam's sin, the ground became cursed. After the fall, it would take "painful toil" to reap necessity from it. Even in our day, the ground in which we live endures curses because of the sins of man.

> 17 To Adam he said, "Because you listened to your wife and ate from the tree about which I commanded you, 'You must not eat of it,' "Cursed is the ground because of you; through painful toil you will eat of it all the days of your life. Genesis 3:17

God confronts sin and demonstrates his method of providing forgiveness and brings people back into fellow ship with him. Out of mercy, an innocent animal's blood covered their sin and clothed their nakedness. Blood to wash away guilt foreshadows the sinless Lamb of God who would pay for the sins of all humanity by his body and blood shed on the cross (Genesis 3:15, John 1:29).

In fact, the law requires that nearly everything be cleansed with blood and without the shedding of blood there is no forgiveness. Hebrews 9:22

Adam and Eve's fall typifies a satanic attack of deception coming from the supernatural realm to destroy God's plans for earth. I do not believe Adam and Eve would have failed God's command without such an attack. Satan seized control of mankind through Adam, who lost his position of authority by transferring to Satan ruler ship over the world in which man lives. They did not understand the importance of God's command until they failed.

Satan did not possess legal authority to rule man's world because God set Adam as the one to rule. Satan could not just come and take Adam's position. Adam had to submit to Satan and reject the command of God, which he did. The first Adam's failure required a second Adam born on earth to redeem mankind. Jesus Christ, the Son of Man, Son of God, became the second Adam born many years later.

# Chapter 7

# Spirit Nature

"I speak the things which I have seen with My Father; therefore you also do the things which you heard from your father." 39 They answered and said to Him, "Abraham is our father." Jesus said to them, "If you are Abraham's children, do the deeds of Abraham. 40 "But as it is, you are seeking to kill Me, a man who has told you the truth, which I heard from God; this Abraham did not do. 41 "You are doing the deeds of your father." They said to Him, "We were not born of fornication; we have one Father: God." 42 Jesus said to them, "If God were your Father, you would love Me, for I proceeded forth and have come from God, for I have not even come on My own initiative, but He sent Me. 43 "Why do you not understand what I am saying? It is because you cannot hear My word. 44 "You are of your father the devil, and you want to do the desires of your father. He was a murderer from the beginning, and does not stand in the truth because there is no truth in him. Whenever he speaks a lie, *he speaks from his own nature,* or he is a liar and the father of lies. 45 "But because I speak the truth, you do not believe Me. 46 "Which one of you convicts Me of sin? If I speak truth, why do you not believe Me? 47 "He who is of God hears the words of God; for this reason you do not hear them, because you are not of God." John 8:38-47 NASB

"You are of your father the devil, and you want to do the desires of your father. He was a murderer from the beginning, and does not stand in the truth because there is no truth in him. *Whenever he speaks a lie, he speaks from his own nature, for he is a liar and the father of lies.* John 8:44 NASB

Nature means "The sum of qualities and attributes; one's native character."[23] True children of God reflect their Heavenly Father's nature, likewise children of the devil reflect his.

> . . . the whole world is under the control of the evil one. 1 John 5:19b

The Greek word for father, patros, metaphorically means an originator of a family who infuses his own spirit into others, who actuates and governs their minds (John 8:44).[24] Satan became the spiritual father of the world and its system (including mankind) by imparting his fallen nature to Adam and Eve through sin.

> [1]AND YOU [He made alive], when you were dead (slain) by [your] trespasses and

sins ²In which at one time you walked [habitually]. **You were following the course and fashion of this world [were under the sway of the tendency of this present age],** following the prince of the power of the air. [You were obedient to and under the control of] the [demon] spirit that still constantly works in the sons of disobedience [the careless, the rebellious, and the unbelieving, who go against the purposes of God].³Among these we as well as you once lived and conducted ourselves in the passions of our flesh **[our behavior governed by our corrupt and sensual nature],** obeying the impulses of the flesh and the thoughts of the mind [our cravings dictated by our senses and our dark imaginings]. We were then by nature children of [God's] wrath and heirs of [His] indignation, like the rest of mankind. Ephesians 2:1-3 Amplified Bible

Satan's nature in mankind, along with fallen spirits, makes it possible for his kingdom to function in and through them. Satan cannot be everywhere at once, but through fallen spirits and fallen people, he does not need to be. They carry out his plans by following their nature under direct influence from his kingdom.

A note in the Book of Enoch indicates the use of the word "Satan" as a title.[25][26] A title is "an inscription or a name by which one is known." [27] Satan is known as the devil. Fallen angels are devils as well. Satan seeks to be glorified, and his spiritual agents want it, too. In direct contrast to the Holy Spirit, Satan's nature produces acts of immorality, impurity, hatred, discord, and rage, while fruit from the nature of God produces love, joy, peace, and kindness, and, when followed, life can be enjoyed.

> So I say, live by the Spirit, and you will not gratify the desires of the sinful nature. For the sinful nature desires what is contrary to the Spirit, and the Spirit what is contrary to the sinful nature. They are in conflict with each other, so that you do not do what you want. But if you are led by the Spirit, you are not under law. The acts of the sinful nature are obvious: sexual immorality, impurity and debauchery; idolatry and witchcraft; hatred, discord, jealousy, fits of rage, selfish ambition, dissensions, factions and envy; drunkenness, orgies, and the like. I warn you, as I did before, that *those who live like this will not inherit the kingdom of God.* But the fruit of the Spirit is love, joy, peace, patience, kindness, goodness, faithfulness, gentleness and self-control. Against such things there is no law. Those who belong to Christ Jesus have crucified the sinful nature with its passions and desires. Since we live by the Spirit, let us keep in step with the Spirit. Galatians 5:16-24

These two kingdoms release their essence or nature flowing from their head. Each kingdom fights for people; God seeks to restore man to eternal life with him through Jesus Christ. Satan fights to keep men trapped far from God to ensure they remain condemned as his for eternity.

# Chapter 8

# Laws of Order

> Thus saith the LORD; If my covenant *be* not with day and night, *and if* I have not appointed the ordinances of heaven and earth. Jeremiah 33:25 KJ

God set creation in order by divine laws. Govern, *memshalah*, denotes "the rule and dominion of God" as used in Genesis 1:16, "God made the sun to govern the day and moon to govern the night."28 Their placement along a twenty-four hour cycle provides a system for time to function on earth.

> "As long as earth endures, seed time and harvest, cold and heat, summer and winter, day and night will never cease" (Gen 8:22). God's laws given by the power of his spoken word keeps all creation functioning. Your laws endure to this day, for all things serve you. Psalm 119:91 (Amplified Bible)

God's statutes govern creation with set order to bring about certain results. For example, reproduction of children requires a male and female; before a harvest of crops, seed must be planted. So we see God's laws produce set results as established by Him.

> . . . Abraham obeyed my voice, and kept my charge, my commandments, my statutes, and my laws. Genesis 26:5 KJV

> . . .and through your offspring all nations on earth will be blessed, because you have obeyed me." Genesis 22:18

> Blessed are they who keep his statutes and seek him with all their heart. Psalm 119:2

When Satan took over rulership of man's world, he knew God's spiritual laws for righteous conduct. If men complied with these laws, they could enjoy relatively decent lives. If ignored, the result would be sin and misery (Exodus 20:1-20, Duet. 28:1-48, Matthew 5:7). God set the norms, and Satan fights them.

To see Satan's kingdom at work, understand the kingdom of God and look for the opposite. As we know, God sets men free, Satan brings bondage. God establishes righteousness; Satan brings the opposite to release destruction and death. A cycle of good and evil repeats itself throughout the generations. [29]

For human relationships, God's set order began with a man and his wife to begin a family. Family displays God's core government structure for human companionship, sexual relationship, and his design to raise children. The family nucleolus works ideally united by love in a committed, submitted relationship to God and each other. As children become adults, families may grow into clans, tribes, and even nations just as Jacob and his offspring became the nation of Israel (Genesis 49).Generations live and die as this cycle repeats, just as seed time and harvest. Satan hates family in the form God established. He seeks to change its divine order to destroy this vital part of God's government structure for mankind.

Nephilim set destructive cycles in motion which aims at destroying families. Deviance from God's set pattern of one man and one woman to form a family entered human behavior. This alteration by the "sons of God" became a direct attack against God's governmental order.

> For this reason a man will leave his father and mother and be united to his wife, and they will become one flesh. Genesis 2:24

Nephilim inject a depth of wickedness that continues to repeat as mankind propels towards the level of corruption as before the flood. Satan seeks to destroy man's obedience to God's laws and decrees, thus causing God's righteous judgment to turn on men who ignore them.

# Chapter 9

# Cain and Able

Woe to them! For they walked in the way of Cain and abandoned themselves for the sake of gain to Balaam's error and perished in Korah's rebellion. Jude 1:11 ESV

Satan's deceptive, religious methods emerged once again to entangle Adam and Eve's offspring. Adam lay with his wife Eve, and she became pregnant and gave birth to Cain. She said, "With the help of the Lord, I have brought forth a man." Later she gave birth to his brother Abel.

Now Abel kept flocks, and Cain worked the soil. In the course of time, Cain brought some of the fruits of the soil as an offering to the Lord. But Abel brought fat portions from some of the firstborn of his flock. The Lord looked with favor on Abel and his offering, but on Cain and his offering, he did not look with favor. So Cain was very angry, and his face was downcast. Then the Lord said to Cain, "Why are you angry? Why is your face downcast? *If you do what is right, will you not be accepted? But if you do not do what is right, sin is crouching at your door; it desires to have you, but you must master it."* Now Cain said to his brother Abel, "Let's go out to the field." And while they were in the field, Cain attacked his brother Abel and killed him. 9Then the LORD said to Cain, "Where is your brother Abel?" "I don't know," he replied. "Am I my brother's keeper?" 10The LORD said, "What have you done? Listen! Your brother's blood cries out to me from the ground.11 Now you are under a curse and driven from the ground, which opened its mouth to receive your brother's blood from your hand. 12When you work the ground, it will no longer yield its crops for you. You will be a restless wanderer on the earth." 13Cain said to the LORD, "My punishment is more than I can bear. 14Today you are driving me from the land, and I will be hidden from your presence; I will be a restless wanderer on the earth, and whoever finds me will kill me." 15But the LORD said to him, "Not so if anyone kills Cain, he will suffer vengeance seven times over." Then the LORD put a mark on Cain so that no one who found him would kill him. 16 So Cain went out from the LORD's presence and lived in the land of Nod, east of Eden (Genesis 4:1-16).

Cain took some not-so-special fruit as an offering for the Lord, while Able gave portions from the firstborn of his flock out of a heart of worship. "Bring the best of the firstfruits of your soil to the house of the LORD your God" (Exodus 23:19).

God seeks worshippers who put him first from their heart. Abel satisfied this requirement, but Cain did not. When a person's spirit does not connect to God, religious activity becomes just that: activity of a religious theme. Cain did this and expected God to bless it, but He didn't and won't. Satan acquired a man who took worship of God away from relationship to one of works. Cain did what seemed acceptable to himself and not to God. He placed his way above God's, exactly what Satan did. To perform religious duties without a spirit united to the Lord's becomes form without substance; flesh without the spirit is dead, and religion without the spirit of God creates activities seemingly serving God, but in reality these systems keep people deceived. Able honored God and gave his offering as an act of worship. Cain performed religious activity, not to honor God but to look like he did. His parents worshiped God through offerings, and Cain knew it would be expected of him. Satan orchestrates dead, man-made religion to keep people trapped in activities far from knowing God.

> But unto Cain and to his offering he had not respect. And Cain was very wroth, and his countenance fell. Genesis 4:5 KJ

Cain's anger burned, stronger and stronger, wroth, in Hebrew, *"charah"* means hot, furious, to burn, kindle with anger.[30] Cain's anger kindled. Why? From the spirit realm, Satan (the tempter) sat at the door of his heart with one goal: to provoke Cain to sin and then seize him for his purposes (1 Thessalonians 3:5).

> ⁶And the Lord said to Cain, Why are you angry? And why do you look sad and depressed and dejected? ⁷If you do well, will you not be accepted? And if you do not do well, sin crouches at your door; its desire is for you, but you must master it" (Genesis 4:6-7) Amplified Bible.
>
> Be ye angry, and sin not: let not the sun go down upon your wrath: Neither give place to the devil. Ephesians 4:26-27

Cain did not master or resist sin, and the rest became history. The devil wants to use our emotions against us. Out of control emotions can be an open door to sin. Thoughts via fiery darts from the spirit realm probably kept stoking the fire of Cain's anger. Foul spirits work to gain strongholds by thoughts and vain imaginations to stir loss of emotional control, then by adding undesirable circumstances emotions inflame creating an atmosphere for sin (Ephesians 6:16).

> 19My dear brothers, take note of this: Everyone should be quick to listen, slow to speak and slow to become angry, 20for man's anger does not bring about the righteous life that God desires. James 1:19

Cain, the first man to fall into the trap of religious dead works, murdered the one who truly worshiped God. A first mention scenario and another cycle that repeats itself on earth as religion murders those who truly worship God because darkness hates the light.

> 11This is the message you heard from the beginning: We should love one another. 12Do not be like Cain, who belonged to the evil one and murdered his brother. And why did he murder him? Because his own actions were evil and his brothers were righteous. 1 John 3:11, 12

Satan successfully seized Cain to move iniquity through his family line, which made a people ripe for his use (Exodus 34:7). Abel's murder stopped him from producing righteous seed, so God gave Adam and Eve another son, Seth, and a new bloodline to produce our Messiah.

> 1This is the written account of Adam's line. When God created man, he made him in the likeness of God. 2He created them male and female and blessed them. And when they were created, he called them "man." 3When Adam had lived 130 years, he had a son in his own likeness, in his own image; and he named him Seth. 4After Seth was born, Adam lived 800 years and had other sons and daughters. 5Altogether, Adam lived 930 years, and then he died. Genesis 5:1-3, 5

Something else we understand about Cain, after he murdered his brother, he left the presence of God. Leaving the presence of the God indicates he previously experienced it.

> And Cain went out from the presence of the LORD, and dwelt in the land of Nod, on the east of Eden. Genesis 4:16 KJV

Cain grew up knowing the Lord but chose sin; his descendants would war with this same option. Adam's creation came in the likeness of God, and Seth came in the likeness and image of his dad, Adam. As Satan set the stage for his next phase of attack, the evil one's plan unfolds to corrupt the seed of man in an attempt to stop the birth of "the seed" (Jesus). Satan already brought death to man's spirit and now murder; he would seek access to the actual DNA of man.

> The LORD God said to the serpent, "Because you have done this, Cursed are you more than all cattle, And more than every beast of the field; On your belly you will go, And dust you will eat All the days of your life; And I will put enmity between you and the woman, And between your seed and her seed; He shall bruise you on the head, And you shall bruise him on the heel." Genesis 3:14-15 NASB

God forespoke in Genesis 3:15 of the serpent's seed who would war against the seed of the woman. "Your seed" in Genesis 3:15 refers to the offspring of Satan, and "her seed," the offspring of the woman who would bruise the head of Satan. In turn, Satan would bruise the heel of the offspring of the woman. We know Jesus provides the crushing blow to Satan, and the "He" who struck his head, but who are the seed of the serpent? Hebrew for seed (zera`) in this scripture means "seed, sowing, offspring, semen virile, descendants, posterity, children." God put hatred in Satan for the woman and her seed. Through the womb of women, Satan sought to destroy her offspring. Adam and Eve's seed were human, so how could Satan have his own "seed"? [31]

In scripture "the seed" came forth by overshadowing of the Holy Spirit (Luke 1:35) with the end result being the physical birth of Jesus from Mary's womb. Recall Cherub angels overshadow the presence of God in the Holy of Holies. Satan as God's mimicker would certainly find a way to have his own "seed."

# Chapter 10

## Corruption of the Seed

> And God looked upon the earth, and, behold, it was corrupt; for all flesh had corrupted his way upon the earth. Genesis 6:12 KJ

Adam and Eve produced daughters somewhere along the way for mankind to multiply on earth. Although scripture does not give us their names, we know daughters were born. Adam and Eve could not produce corrupt seed of their kind after their fall, spiritually dead in sin, but their physical children would be in kind to them.

After Cain, Abel, or Seth's birth, the word corrupt was not used, but after "sons of god" bred with "daughters of men," corruption of all flesh fully permeated earth (Genesis 6:12). Earth became fully contaminated with heartless, wicked, violent people who lacked any normal regard for life. God never formed man with corruption in mind but for righteousness.32 Just who were these "sons of God" and what made them capable of producing such vile offspring? Did Satan entice angels to take "human form" and inject corruption into Adamic seed through daughters of men? Could this really occur when angels possess spirit bodies and humans possess physical bodies? If anything, it would seem to affect only the spirits of humans which Satan already accomplished through Adam and Eve's fall into sin. We must look closely at scripture to see what did happen when "sons of God" produced children with "daughters of men."

# Chapter 11

# Nephilim

> When the wicked are in authority, sin increases. But the godly will live to see the tyrant's downfall. Pro 29:16- New Living Translation

The first mention of the Nephilim occurs in Genesis, chapter 6, where God "grieved for making man" (Gen 6:6). What a drastic change from man's creation to this point in time. As you read, it becomes evident that when the Nephilim show up, the inclination of men's heart turns to wickedness at all times (Gen 6:5). Sons of God took wives from daughters of men who bore offspring so depraved the entire earth came under judgment due to their infusion of evil. These males were not called "sons of men" but "sons of God." I see no need for the writer (Moses) to specifically mention wives being taken here because in verse one; we understand men began to greatly increase upon the earth already, and this cannot occur without female partners. But "sons of God" doing the taking were referenced because they were not ordinary men.

> 1 Now it came about, when men began to multiply on the face of the land, and daughters were born to them, 2 that the sons of God saw that the daughters of men were beautiful; and they took wives for themselves, whomever they chose. 3 Then the LORD said, "My Spirit shall not strive with man forever, because he also is flesh; nevertheless his days shall be one hundred and twenty years." 4 The Nephilim were on the earth in those days, and also afterward, when the sons of God came in to the daughters of men, and they bore children to them. Those were the mighty men who were of old, men of renown. 5 Then the LORD saw that the wickedness of man was great on the earth, and that every intent of the thoughts of his heart was only evil continually. 6 The LORD was sorry that He had made man on the earth, and He was grieved in His heart. Genesis 6:1-6 NASB

Some Bible translations use "giants" in place of "Nephilim," such as the Amplified Bible Translation.

> 4There were giants on the earth in those days- -and also afterward--when the sons of God lived with the daughters of men, and they bore children to them. These were the mighty men who were of old, men of renown. Genesis 6:4 Amplified Bible

Looking through scripture to determine the identity of these "sons of God" finds the Book of Job with two occurrences of "sons of God" in which they are both angels.

> Now there was a day when the *sons of God* came to present themselves before the LORD, and Satan came also among them. Job 1:6 KJ

> Again there was a day when the *sons of God* came to present themselves before the LORD, and Satan came also among them to present himself before the LORD. Job 2:1 KJ

Elsewhere in the Old Testament, God references his children as "sons and daughters" (Is. 43:6; 45:11). Years forward to the New Testament we find those whose faith in Jesus Christ, the Son of God, born of the Virgin Mary, crucified, buried and resurrected from the dead, ascended to the Heavenly Father, produces sons (and daughters) of God, who are led by the Spirit of God.

> 3 For I delivered to you as of first importance what I also received, that Christ died for our sins according to the Scriptures, 4 and that He was buried, and that He was raised on the third day according to the Scriptures.1 Corinthians 15:3-4 NASB

> For you are all sons of God through faith in Christ Jesus. Galatians 3:26 NASB

> 12Yet to all who received him, to those who believed in his name, he gave the right to become children of God 13children born not of natural descent, nor of human decision or a husband's will, but born of God. John 1:12-13 NASB

> 13 for if you are living according to the flesh, you must die; but if by the Spirit you are putting to death the deeds of the body, you will live. 14 For all who are being led by the Spirit of God, these are sons of God. Romans 8:13-14 NASB

Biblical translations of Deuteronomy 32:8 derived from Masoretic Texts states, "God divided earth and gave boundaries to the nations according to the sons of Israel." With the discovery of the Dead Sea Scrolls, a more accurate translation of this verse was found. [33] The New Living Bible reflects this recently discovered translation.

> When the Most High assigned lands to the nations, when he divided up the human race, he established the boundaries of the peoples according to the number in his heavenly court. [a] Deuteronomy 32:8 NLT

> [a] As in Dead Sea Scrolls, which read *the number of the sons of God,* and Greek version, which reads *the number of the angels of God;* Masoretic Text reads *the number of the sons of Israel.*

God assigned lands to nations and people according to the number "sons of god" or angels. The best explanation of Genesis, chapter six, sons of God" points to angels.

One hindrance for grasping this point comes with the topic of angels marrying. No reason exists for angels to marry at any time; God brought forth their number in totality at creation with no need or command to reproduce. Marriage symbolizes a believer's union with the Lord and deals with a man and wife's covenant relationship for their lives on earth. Jesus tells us angels in heaven do not marry, and we believe him, so in Matthew 22:30, Jesus' response corresponds to the Sadducees (who did not believe in the resurrection) and a question about marriage at the resurrection, not the issue of rebellious angels and what they did.

> That same day the Sadducees, who say there is no resurrection, came to him with a question. "Teacher," they said, "Moses told us that if a man dies without having children, his brother must marry the widow and have children for him. Now there were seven brothers among us. The first one married and died, and since he had no children, he left his wife to his brother. The same thing happened to the second and third brother, right on down to the seventh. Finally, the woman died. Now then, at the resurrection, whose wife will she be of the seven, since all of them were married to her?" Jesus replied, You are in error because you do not know the Scriptures or the power of God. At the resurrection people will neither marry nor be given in marriage; they will be like the angels in heaven. Matthew 22:23-30

The Book of Jude from the New Testament writes of angels who abandoned their first position.

> 6And the angels who did not keep their positions of authority but abandoned their own home—these he has kept in darkness, bound with everlasting chains for judgment on the great Day. In a similar way, Sodom and Gomorrah and the surrounding towns gave themselves up to sexual immorality and perversion. They serve as an example of those who suffer the punishment of eternal fire. Jude 1:6-7

> And the angels which kept not their first estate, but left their own habitation, he hath reserved in everlasting chains under darkness unto the judgment of the great day. Even as Sodom and Gomorrah, and the cities about them in like manner, giving themselves over to fornication, and going after strange flesh, are set forth for an example, suffering the vengeance of eternal fire. Jude 1:6-7 KJV

Certain angels did not keep their first place of authority in service to God and left their own habitation. "Habitation" (oiketerion) means a dwelling place or figuratively "the body" as a dwelling place for the spirit. Fallen angels of Genesis 6 left their original state to enter the physical realm and take the likeness of human men to engage in sexual relations with the daughters of men. Like those from Sodom and Gomorrah, these angels went after strange flesh giving themselves over to fornication. 2 Corinthians 5:2 uses the same Greek word (oiketerion) for house, as a body.
[34]

> For in this we groan, earnestly desiring to be clothed upon with our house which is from heaven . . . 2 Cor 5:2 KJV

> We grow weary in our present bodies, and we long for the day when we will put on our heavenly bodies like new clothing. 2 Cor. 5:2 NLT

> Peter, the apostle, also tells us, "Angels sinned."4 For if God did not spare angels when they sinned, but cast them into hell and committed them to pits of darkness, reserved for judgment; 2 Peter 2:4 NASB

In scripture angels appear as men to relay a message from God to Abraham, Moses, Ezekiel, Daniel, Samson's mother, and Mary, to name a few. A dimension exists where angels appear and vanish from our sight. We also find angels taking the form of men: eating, drinking, talking, wrestling, and the like, occurring by physical interaction just as human to human. On one mission from God, angels looked human to all the men of Sodom (Genesis, Chapters18 and 19).

> Then the men turned away from there and went toward Sodom, while Abraham was still standing before the LORD. Upon entering Sodom two angels received an invitation to spend the night at Lot's house. Genesis 18:22 NIV

> 1 The *two angels* arrived at Sodom in the evening, and Lot was sitting in the gateway of the city. When he saw them, he got up to meet them and bowed down with his face to the ground. 2 "*My lords*," he said, "please turn aside to your servant's house. You can wash your feet and spend the night and then go on your way early in the morning." "No," they answered, "we

will spend the night in the square." 3 But he insisted so strongly that they did go with him and entered his house. He prepared a meal for them, baking bread without yeast, and they ate. 4 Before they had gone to bed, all the men from every part of the city of Sodom—both and old—surrounded the house. 5 They called to Lot, "*Where are the men who came to you tonight?* Bring them out to us *so that we can have sex with them*." 6 Lot went outside to meet them and shut the door behind him 7 and said, "No, my friends. Don't do this wicked thing. 8 Look, I have two daughters who have never slept with a man. Let me bring them out to you, and you can do what you like with them. But don't do anything to *these men*, for they have come under the protection of my roof." "Get out of our way," they replied. And they said, "This fellow came here as an alien, and now he wants to play the judge! We'll treat you worse than them." They kept bringing pressure on Lot and moved forward to break down the door.10 But *the men* inside reached out and pulled Lot back into the house and shut the door. 11 Then they struck the men who were at the door of the house, young and old, with blindness so that they could not find the door.12 *The two men* said to Lot, "Do you have anyone else here—sons-in-law, sons or daughters, or anyone else in the city who belongs to you? Get them out of here, 13 because we are going to destroy this place. The outcry to the LORD against its people is so great that he has sent us to destroy it." 14

> So Lot went out and spoke to his sons-in-law, who were pledged to marry] his daughters. He said, "Hurry and get out of this place, because the LORD is about to destroy the city!" But his sons-in-law thought he was joking.15With the coming of dawn, the angels urged Lot, saying, "Hurry! Take your wife and your two daughters who are here, or you will be swept away when the city is punished." Genesis 9:1-5

Initially, Lot did not know angels were before him and addressed them as lord, a Hebrew term *"adown"* for men.[35] That night all the men from Sodom called to Lot, "Where are the men who came to you tonight? Bring them out to us so that we can have sex with them" (Genesis 19:5). Clearly, we see two angels arriving at Sodom, having feet to wash, and in need of a place to sleep, just as humans. These angels looked like men, so much so that the Sodomites wanted to have sex with them. It seems angels taking the form of human men had bodies capable of engaging in sex; those outside Lot's house thought so. Mere men cannot strike a mob with blindness or bring destruction to Sodom and Gomorrah, but angels with supernatural ability can.

> The *fallen ones* were in the earth in those days, and even after wards when sons of God come in unto daughters of men, and they have borne to them -- they are the heroes, who, from of old, are the men of name. Genesis 6:4 Young's Literal Translation

The ancient Book of Enoch states "sons of God" were Watcher angels who deserted heaven and polluted them- selves with women. This reveals the origins of evil spirits that walk the earth.

## Help from the Book of Enoch

1 And He answered and said to me, and I heard His voice: 'Fear not, Enoch, thou righteous 2 man and scribe of righteousness: approach hither and hear my voice. And go, say to the Watchers of heaven, who have sent thee to intercede for them: "You should intercede" for men, and not men 3 for you: Wherefore have ye left the high, holy, and eternal heaven, and lain with women, and defiled yourselves with the daughters of men and taken to yourselves wives, and done like the children 4 of earth, and begotten giants (as your) sons? And though ye were holy, spiritual, living the eternal life, you have defiled yourselves with the blood of women, and have begotten (children) with the blood of flesh, and, as the children of men, have lusted after flesh and blood as those also do who die 5 and perish. Therefore have I given them wives also that they might impregnate them, and beget 6 children by them, that thus nothing might be wanting to them on earth. But you were formerly 7 spiritual, living the eternal life, and immortal for all generations of the world. And therefore I have not appointed wives for you; for as for the spiritual ones of the heaven, in heaven is their dwelling. 8 And now, the giants, who are produced from the spirits

and flesh, shall be called evil spirits upon 9 the earth, and on the earth shall be their dwelling. Evil spirits have proceeded from their bodies; because they are born from men and from the holy Watchers is their beginning and primal origin; 10 they shall be evil spirits on earth, and evil spirits shall they be called. [As for the spirits of heaven, in heaven shall be their dwelling, but as for the spirits of the earth which were born upon the earth, on the earth shall be their dwelling.] And the spirits of the giants afflict, oppress, destroy, attack, do battle, and work destruction on the earth, and cause trouble: they take no food, but nevertheless 12 hunger and thirst, and cause offences. And these spirits shall rise up against the children of men and against the women, because they have proceeded from them." [36] [37]

# Chapter 12

# Where on Earth?

Where did the sons of God begin their encroachment on earth? Chapter 7 of the Book of Enoch informs us this occurred on Mt. Armon, also known as Mount Hermon, located in the Middle East.

> Book of Enoch Chapter 7
>
> 1It happened after the sons of men had multiplied in those days, that daughters were born to them, elegant and beautiful.2And when the angels, the sons of heaven, beheld them, they became enamored of them, saying to each other, Come, let us select for ourselves wives from the progeny of men, and let us beget children.3Then their leader Samyaza said to them; I fear that you may perhaps be indisposed to the performance of this enterprise; 4And that I alone shall suffer for so grievous a crime.5But they answered him and said; We all swear;6And bind ourselves by mutual execrations, that we will not change

our intention, but execute our projected undertaking.7Then they swore all together, and all bound themselves by mutual execrations. Their whole number was two hundred, who descended upon Ardis, which is the top of mount Armon.[38]

Early religious activity around Mount Hermon involved "worship of mythology gods with such practices as divination, magic, astrology, animal and human sacrifices, purification rites and the like."[39] Almost two dozen ancient temples have been found on or near Mount Hermon. All line up with practices taught by the Nephilim. "With the history of this region, the onslaught of the rebellious sons of god surely came about here." [40] Mythology in itself is full of half human and half god characters. A demigod according to mythology is "a half god, or an inferior deity; the offspring of a deity and a mortal."[41] One of the oldest pieces of literature discovered came from Mesopotamia. In the Sumerian *Epic of Gilgamesh,* 'his father was Lugalbanda and his mother was Ninsun (whom some call Rimat Ninsun), a goddess. In Mesopotamian mythology, Gilgamesh is a demigod of super-human ability usually described as two-thirds god and one third man."[42] These people were drawn to stories like this because of their Nephilim ancestry and the work of diabolical spirits.

# Chapter 13

# Revealed in Ancient Hebrew

Looking at the letters making up the Hebrew word for "life" reveals a clear distinction when it comes to the Nephilim. In their book *Devils and Demons and the Return of the Nephilim,* John Klein and Adam Spears explain what this means.

> "In general, the Hebrew word *chai* means 'life," but *chai* can be spelled in three different ways, with each spelling referring to a distinct type of life. The first way to spell chai, uses the Hebrew characters *chey-yod-yod.* Pictographically, this is a picture of God putting a fense (chet) aroung His work (yod). This fence of protection encloses God's orderly creation and prevents chaos from entering. Biologically speaking, without these fences of protection life cannot last very long: for example, the cell wall of the skin that covers our bodies provide irreplaceable protection.

The first yod, pictographically, represents the work of God. The second yod explains how He made it, by forming it with His own hand and breathing life into it. In this creation passage, God was revealing the nature of the unique and intimate relationship He was proposing to have with mankind. He was further affirming that man is separate and distinct from all other kinds of life, made by God's hand in His own image, with his life literally "breathed in" by God. This word also correlates to (i.e., symbolically signifies) the Hebrew word, *nishmah*, which ancient rabbis spoke about as representing the spark of God that dwells within each human.

The second way of spelling chai uses the Hebrew characters *chet-yod,* which references the Hebrew word "nefash." Nefash means "all other life that God spoke forth." This stands in contrast to the only form of life that He literally formed with His own hands. This spelling can be used for all life of any kind, including man and animals. It refers to all life in existence – everything that's alive. The one yod represents the work that God did in making this kind of life. . .He spoke it forth and put a fence of protection around it as well.

The third way to spell *chai* uses only the Hebrew letter *chet.* This spelling contains no yod (work of God) at all, meaning that both *God's work and His spirit are completely absent from it.* Yet oddly enough, it still designates "a living thing." This usage of chet is limited to Nephilim only, but has sometimes been translated as "evil beast," presumably to avoid confusion with a "wild beast" such as a lion or bear. Finally, here's one more very revealing distinction. The Hebrew letters for the word nephal (singular for Nephilim) are nun-pay- lamed, which pictographically means "to speak control over life." [43]

We're talking about angels who apostatized and left their holy assignment. As Satan's angels, these "sons of God" reflect him in depravity and action. Considering Satan's purposes, along with his angelic army in destroying God's kingdom and especially his hatred for man in his image, why would he not seek a means to corrupt the "promise of God" (Genesis 1:27, 3:15). He would accomplish this goal by actually corrupting the physical seed of man. After all, we know Satan's seed would attack the seed of the woman, and by polluting her actual "seed," those genes would thread through the generations of mankind. Each of these defiling angels sought to engender children and especially sons. In Satan's quest "to be like God," he sought his own "seed" of humans through whom he could rule and control earth.

Some think it is not likely that apostate angels produced offspring with human females because of previous stated difference in angels and humans, and by the fact we do not see giants as in Biblical days (Deut. 3:11). I understand, but in their apostasy, angels took the "form of men," and as Nephilim, inbred their size which altered through the generations. I challenge the reader to do an Internet search on large skeletal remains found throughout history, as these align with Biblical accounts of the existence of giants.

> And the angels who did not keep their positions of authority but abandoned their own home--these he has kept in darkness, bound with everlasting chains for judgment on the great Day. Jude 1:6

Jude 1:6 would be the logical reason we do not see giants that size as in scripture. God cast them into darkness and bound them with chains of constraint, which kept them from fornication as they did before. God's sentence of judgment left an example of what would happen to any other angel who thought about it. Another theory the reader may consider is that these angels are bound by the constraints of chains and prisoners of earth's judgment (darkness), kept from heaven and fornication, but while under the sentence of judgment, they move about the realms of earth. Spirits in the abyss do come out by the will of God to perform certain tasks (Revelations, chapter 9).Satan's angels are under judgment from God and await a judgment day. But until that time, the majority of them roam earth realms (Jude 1:6). Some selections from the Book of Enoch provide the reasoning for this line of thinking.

> [5]Then *the Lord* said to me: Enoch, scribe of righteousness, go tell the Watchers of heaven, who have deserted the lofty sky, and their holy everlasting station, *who* have been polluted with women. [6]And have done as the sons of men do, by taking to themselves wives, and *who* have been greatly corrupted on the earth; [7]That on the earth they shall never obtain peace and remission of sin. For they shall not rejoice in their offspring; they shall behold the slaughter of their beloved; shall lament for the destruction of their sons; and shall

> petition for ever; but shall not obtain mercy and peace. ¹Then Enoch, passing on, said to Azazyel: You shalt not obtain peace. A great sentence is gone forth against you. *He shall bind you; ²Neither shall relief, mercy, and supplication be yours, on account of the oppression which you have taught; ³And on account of every act of blasphemy, tyranny, and sin, which you have discovered to the children of men.* ³Judgment has been passed upon you: *your request* will not be granted you. *⁴From this time forward, never shall you ascend into heaven; He has said that on the earth He will bind you, as long as the world endures.* Book of Enoch, Chapter 12 -13; 14:3-4 ⁴⁴

After his resurrection, Jesus went to preach to disobedient spirits in prison from before the flood. Who were these spirits?

> For Christ died for sins once for all, the righteous for the unrighteous, to bring you to God. He was put to death in the body but made alive by the Spirit, 19through whom also he went and preached to the spirits in prison 20who disobeyed long ago when God waited patiently in the days of Noah while the ark was being built. 1 Peter 3:18-19

"Spirits in prison" in this scripture probably were that of humans who chose to "disobey" and partake of the same sins of the Nephilim prior to the flood. Fallen angels, along with their offspring, could have also been a part of this audience. The word for "spirits" in 1 Peter 3:19, *pneuma,* translates as the spirit of a human, angel, or of God.[45] Jesus' triumphant victory and his authority over sin and death were on display to every one of these spiritual prisoners with his proclamation of victory.

Demonic spirits may oppress people sexually but are not able to create children since they are spirits and do not have the capability to do so. After the fallen angels who produced the Nephilim became chained in darkness, their ability to take on the form of human males and conceive additional first generation giants stopped, thank God!

Allow me to introduce two terms for the study in this book: "Seed of the Nephilim" and those "seeded" by the influence of a Nephilim spirits." A "seed of the Nephilim" carries genetics of the Nephilim in their body. Nephilim genetics pass down through family lines along with Nephilim spirits. People "seeded" under the influence of Nephilim are those enticed and afflicted by these demons and devils who continue their assault against mankind from the spirit realm. Seed of the Nephilim are the same as Satan's seed spoken of in Genesis 3:15.

Scripturally, we do see that genetics of giants pass down to their descendants. Anak (neck) was the progenitor of a family, or tribe of giants from Hebron.[46] They went up through the Negev and came to Hebron, where Ahiman, Sheshai and Talmai, the descendants of Anak, lived. Numbers 13:22a

"Seeded" individuals will be under the effect of a Nephilim spirit and may even house these spirits due to unrepentant sins and agreement with them. Upon true repentance and forgiveness provided through Jesus Christ, seeded people can be totally delivered. True seed of the Nephilim will not repent. If it seems they do, it is a pretense.

A challenge exists to determine if a person is a true seed of a Nephilim or one seeded under the influence of these spirits. God knows the difference, and those led by the Holy Spirit will receive understanding from him as to what they are dealing with in a given situation.

An example of people seeded and succumbed by Nephilim spirits would be Israel when they disobeyed God and came under the influence of the Nephilim nations and acted just as they did.

> You not only walked in their ways and copied their detestable practices, but in all your ways you soon became more depraved than they. Ezekiel 16:47

# Chapter 14

# Defining to Expose

4 The Nephilim were on the earth in those days, and also afterward, when the sons of God came in to the daughters of men, and they bore children to them. Those were the mighty men who were of old, men of renown. Genesis 6:4

Nephilim (Hebrew) means "violent or causing to fall." "Nephilim were violent tyrants, who fell upon others. The word may also be derived from a root signifying "wonder," and hence "monsters" or "prodigies." [47,48]

Nephilim (giants) are the children of "sons of God" and "daughters of men" known as "mighty men," "who were of old," "men of renown" (Genesis 6:4). A breakdown of these three descriptive phrases reveals pertinent information needed to understand the Nephilim.

The Hebrew word "gibbowr" (Strongs #1368) for "mighty men" first appears in Genesis 6:4 defined as "powerful; by implication, warrior, tyrant -- champion, chief, excel, giant, man, mighty (man, one), strong (man), valiant man." [49] Used 68 times in the Old Testament, "mighty men" consists of both righteous and unrighteous connotations. The word refers to a class of "fighting men" or "warriors." In a righteous sense, Joshua and King David were mighty men of battle, and leaders of others the same (Josh. 1:14; 2 Sam.23).[50]

The next phrase for Nephilim, "who were of old" from (Strongs #5769) a Hebrew word, "olam" meaning "what is hidden, of time long past, perpetuity, concealed, i.e. the vanishing point; with a short definition, of forever or eternity. [51] Sons of God and their offspring would possess origins from eternity.

> Yes, what sorrow awaits you! For you are like hidden graves in a field. People walk over them without knowing the corruption they are stepping on." Luke 11:44 NLT

*Alam* (Strong's H5956 ), the Hebrew root word for *Owlam,* gives more details to grasp just what we are dealing with concerning the seed of the Nephilim. *Alam* means to conceal, hide, be hidden, be concealed, be secret, to hide oneself, dissembler.[52] Now let's define dissemble: 1) to give a false or misleading appearance; to conceal the truth or real nature of; 2) to conceal one's true motives, thoughts, etc., by some pretense; speak or act hypocritically. Next add synonyms for dissemble: mask, hide, camouflage, and we discover how seed of the Nephilim act in our midst.[53]

Let's read another Biblical account of the appearance of an angel perceived to be a "man." Notice this angel appears and delivers his message and disappears into a vanishing point in the flames.

> 2There was a certain man of Zorah, of the family of the Danites, whose name was Manoah; and his wife was barren and had borne no children. *3Then the angel of the LORD appeared to the woman and said to her,* "Behold now, you are barren and have borne no children, but you shall conceive and give birth to a son. 4"Now therefore, be careful not to drink wine or strong drink, nor eat any unclean thing. 5"For behold, you shall conceive and give birth to a son, and no razor shall come upon his head, for the boy shall be a Nazirite to God from the womb; and he shall begin to deliver Israel from the hands of the Philistines." 6Then the woman came and told her husband, saying, *"A man of God came to me and his appearance was like the appearance of the angel of God, very awesome.* And I did not ask him where he came from, nor did he tell me his name. 7"But he said to me, 'Behold, you shall conceive and give birth to a son, and now you shall not drink wine or strong drink nor eat any unclean thing, for the boy shall be a Nazirite to God from the womb to the day of his death.'"8Then Manoah entreated the LORD and said, "O Lord, please let the *man of God* whom You have sent come to us again that he may teach us what to do for the boy who is to be born."

9God listened to the voice of Manoah; and the angel of God came again to the woman as she was sitting in the field, but Manoah her husband was not with her. 10So the woman ran quickly and told her husband, "Behold, the man who came the other day has appeared to me." 11Then Manoah arose and followed his wife, and when he came to the man he said to him, "Are you the man who spoke to the woman?" And he said, "I am." 12Manoah said, "Now when your words come to pass, what shall be the boy's mode of life and his vocation?" 13So the angel of the LORD said to Manoah, "Let the woman pay attention to all that I said. 14"She should not eat anything that comes from the vine nor drink wine or strong drink, nor eat any unclean thing; let her observe all that I commanded." 15Then Manoah said to the angel of the LORD, "Please let us detain you so that we may prepare a young goat for you." 16The angel of the LORD said to Manoah, "Though you detain me, I will not eat your food, but if you prepare a burnt offering, then offer it to the LORD." For Manoah did not know that he was the angel of the LORD. 17Manoah said to the angel of the LORD, "What is your name, so that when your words come to pass, we may honor you?" 18But the angel of the LORD said to him, "Why do you ask my name, seeing it is wonderful?" 19So Manoah took the young goat with the grain offering and offered it on the rock to the LORD, and He performed wonders while Manoah and his wife looked on. 20For it came about when the flame went up from the altar toward heaven that the angel of the LORD ascended in the flame of the altar. When Manoah and his wife saw this, they fell on their faces to the ground. Judges 13:2-20 NIV

Manoah and his wife interact with this angel. Only when the angel ascends in the flames do they realize he was not a "man" but an actual angel from the Lord.

The last phrase, "men of renown," reveals the Nephilim were known or famous, which can be understood by one of three Hebrew words for Nephilim: "naphal,"meaning "a feller, a bully or a tyrant -- giant." 54Nephilim became famous because they were fellers, bullies, and tyrants. 55 Feller defined "fierce; cruel; dreadful, destructive; deadly, savage, along with synonyms of barbaric, unrestrained, inhuman and inhumane" to name a few indicates what they were known for.56

A bully is a "quarrelsome, overbearing person who habitually badgers and intimidates smaller or weaker people."57 Does it seem that our current culture has an epidemic of bullying? At times bullying drives weak victims to destruction because of their unrelenting taunts. I recall a news story of a young victim of bullying that continued on social networks. After the victim's death by suicide, these bullies continued to taunt the victim's memorial with absolutely no mercy.

A tyrant is one who uses oppression to dominate others. "Specifically, a tyrant is a ruler who uses power to oppress his subjects; a person who exercises authority in an unlawful manner; one who by taxation, injustice, or cruel punishment, or the demand of unreasonable services, imposes burdens and hardships on those under his control; a cruel master; an oppressor." [58] "In the exact sense, a tyrant arrogates to him or herself royal authority without having a right to it. This is how the Greeks understood the word 'tyrant': they applied it indifferently to good and bad princes whose authority was not legitimate." [59] This brings out the elitism by which the Nephilim exalt themselves above others. Whether or not they truly are royalty, in their own minds they are, with others made subject to them. Another term for a tyrant, despot or a dictator, exposes the manner by which these people rise and seize power.

> 24 "Can the prey be taken from the mighty man, Or the captives of a tyrant be rescued?" 25 Surely, thus says the LORD, "Even the captives of the mighty man will be taken away, And the prey of the tyrant will be rescued; For I will contend with the one who contends with you, And I will save your sons. 26 "I will feed your oppressors with their own flesh, And they will become drunk with their own blood as with sweet wine; And all flesh will know that I, the LORD, am your Savior And your Redeemer, the Mighty One of Jacob." Isaiah 49:24-26 NASB

Tyrants and bullies seek control as Nephilim want power over others. "Nephal, (singular) for Nephilim, means a living abortion."[60] An abortion terminates life; similarly Nephilim lack the full essence of human life. Abortion can also mean a malformed or monstrous person or thing.[61] By definitions and synonyms for monster, we get some more understanding of the Nephilim. They are monsters and, interestingly, a monster is a supernatural being and the root of this problem. Monster means "Anything or a person of unnatural or excessive ugliness, deformity, wickedness, or cruelty."[62]

> There were giants in the earth in those days; and also after that, when the sons of God came in unto the daughters of men, **and they bare [children] to them, the same** [became] mighty men which [were] of old, men of renown. Genesis 6:4 KJV

Using the King James Bible, we see the children of "sons of Gods" were the same as the "sons of God." Why? Because the daughters of men were the ones baring the children, and the children they bore were the same as their fathers (sons of gods). Their fathers were devils or angels in rebellion to God, and so are their offspring. So we can say Nephilim turn out to be like their fathers, devils in the flesh.

# Chapter 15

# Deviation

Life before the flood deviated far from what God envisioned. When "sons of God" defiled themselves with females, their corrupt offspring arose. With longevity of human life at this point, Adam and Eve's offspring reproduced enough children for mankind to multiply (Genesis 6:1). Giants appeared on planet earth much sooner than we may think. "Sons of God" fornicated with "daughters of men" early on because the scripture says, "**when** man began to multiple, the sons of God took notice of daughters of men (Genesis 6:2)." In this verse, Moses introduced the problem: not only did human males bred with human females, "sons of God" also took human females as wives and produced offspring. Here we understand "men" and "sons of God" were making babies.

> The sons of God saw the beautiful women and took any they wanted as their wives.
> Genesis 6:2 NLT

Sons of God took any female they decided upon and as many as they wanted. Even if she was not agreeable, it did not matter. According to the Book of Enoch, these angels knew it was a grievous sin but did it anyway. Fallen angels and their offspring continued to have sex with many women, creating more and more Nephilim seeded humans.

## Originators of Sexual Perversions

These sons of God introduced sexual perversion to earth. Why perversion? Because angels were not authorized by God's to engage in sex or reproduction. They perverted and distorted the natural order of sexual relationships set by God. This opened the door to multiple sex partners and sexual perversion. Sons of God took many females for sex, whether by seduction or rape. Harems can be traced back to this Nephilim influence.[63]

Sons of God and their Nephilim offspring were seducers of females. In turn, the females became seducers of males. Furthermore, Nephilim led the way to establish other forms of sexual perversion. We know this by the cities of Sodom and Gomorrah which were Canaanite cities of Nephilim descent. Men turned away from natural sexual relationships to burn with passion towards one another. As Nephilim, their sexual lust would be satisfied according to their desires, regardless of anyone else. Others are used for their pleasure, including young children, boys or girls, and animals. We find Nephilim spirits at work through sexual perversion.

# Chapter 16

# Corrupt Seed

Satan entered mankind bringing spiritual death via Adam and Eve. The "sons of God" entered flesh of mankind through sexual intercourse to bring corruption into the physical seed of man. Angels posing as men could not produce pure Adamic seed. Seed or sperm released by these "sons of God" produced altered humans. A mingled or diverse seed was forbidden in the Bible (Leviticus 19:19). Through the "sons of God" abnormalities entered into human genetics which added physical and psychosocial obstruction to already spiritually dead humans. Satan achieved corruptive damage to humans in spirit, soul, and body.

Nephilim genetics continued to be bred into more humans as they spread throughout the earth. Not until "sons of God" produced children did the word "corrupt" describe the human condition on earth.

So we see two types of humans were conceived on earth, one of Adam's stock and the other a mixed seed of the "sons of God" with "daughters of men." As a result "the Lord said, 'My spirit shall not always strive with man, for that he also is flesh: yet his days shall be an hundred and twenty years' " (Genesis 6:3 KJ). Earth changed because of the "sons of God" invasion. God's response was to put a limit on man's days, and how long he would contend with them.

> 5The Lord saw how great man's wickedness on the earth had become, and that every inclination of the thoughts of his heart was only evil all the time. Genesis 6:5

The thoughts of mankind's heart had not been described in this manner before Genesis 6. After "sons of God" reproduced in humans, "every inclination of the thoughts of man's heart was only evil all the time" (Genesis 6:5). God's response was He repented for making man and prepared for judgment.

> 6And it repented the LORD that he had made man on the earth, and it grieved him at his heart. 7And the LORD said, I will destroy man whom I have created from the face of the earth; both man, and beast, and the creeping thing, and the fowls of the air; for it repenteth me that I have made them. Genesis 6:5 KJ

These "sons of God" followed Satan in rebellion and became a god unto themselves. Let's think this out. The form angels took was of human men, but in reality they were not men but posed as men. They were deceivers, impostors, and fakes. Rebel angels' corralled earth for sex, introduced sexual perversion to man's population, and produced abnormal humans. God authorizes holy angels to take on the form of men, but rebel angels perverted themselves to corrupt life on earth. Pervert means to affect with perversion, lead astray morally, turn away from the right course, or lead into mental error or false judgment.[64]

## Chapter 17

## Blending In

Let's look at the first four generations of Nephilim, and how they blended into mankind. The first generation would be the parents themselves who are the "sons of God" and "daughters of men."

> There were giants in the earth in those days; and also after that, when the sons of God came in unto the daughters of men, and they bore children to them, the same became mighty men which were of old, men of renown. Genesis 6:4 KJ

Their children, the second generation, were called the Nephilim or Giants. Next, the third generation became known as "mighty men." By interbreeding with humans, a blending into Adam's seed took place. Their genes did as well, and at this point they were called "*men*." With continued interbreeding they looked just like any other man, woman, or child. This phrase "mighty men were of old," meaning the seed of the Nephilim, had been around for a long time while interbreeding and blending into the normal population.

By the time of Genesis 6:4, generations had already multiplied with corruption and giants of evil already blended into men. Recall, the root word for Nephilim, alam, "means hidden or concealed," and for generations the Nephilim interbred with the seed of woman and became hidden.[65] Nephilim are wired to conceal themselves, their true motives, and their true intent. They are drawn to darkness because darkness is natural to them. Righteousness is unnatural but a pretense of righteousness works for them. They are natural pretenders who blend into society perpetuating hell on earth. As tools of Satan, they release harm, death and destruction to the normal population.

# Chapter 18

## Tools for their Seed

And all the others together with them took unto themselves wives, and each chose for himself one, and they began to go in unto them and to defile themselves with them, and they taught them charms and enchantments, and the cutting of roots, and made them acquainted with plants. 2. And they became pregnant, and they bare great giants, whose height was three thousand ells: Book of Enoch 7:1-2 [66]

Then they took wives, each choosing for himself; whom they began to approach, and with whom they cohabited; teaching them sorcery, incantations, and the dividing of roots and trees. Book of Enoch 7:10 [67]

Semjaza taught enchantments, and root-cuttings, 'Armaros the resolving of enchantments, Baraqijal (taught) astrology, Kokabel the constellations, Ezeqeel the knowledge of the clouds, Araqiel the signs of the earth, Shamsiel the signs of the sun, and Sariel the course of the moon. Book of Enoch 8:3 [68]

Defiling and teaching "witchcraft, charms, enchantments, cutting of roots, sorcery, astrology, divination, acquainting them with plants and signs of the earth, all going hand in hand as tools in satanic purposes," (Book of Enoch 7:1). These practices taught daughters of men and their offspring how to participate with spiritual forces of evil. Each one of these females became an open door for a devil to access her physically and spiritually. When a devil no longer appeared as a human man, it still had access to her because of her spiritual union with it.

Sons of gods also taught the exaltation of devils as gods which gained human participation through idolatrous, pagan religious systems. W.E. Vine's M.A., Expository Dictionary of New Testament Words expands our understanding.

SORCERY

"1. *pharmakia* (or *eia*) (φαρμακεία, 5331) (Eng., "pharmacy," etc.) primarily signified "the use of medicine, drugs, spells"; then, "poisoning"; then, "sorcery," Gal. 5:20, "sorcery" (KJV, "witchcraft"), mentioned as one of "the works of the flesh." See also Rev. 9:21; 18:23. In the Sept., Ex. 7:11, 22; 8:7, 18; Isa. 47:9, 12, in "sorcery," use of drugs, whether simple or potent, generally accompanied by incantations and appeals to occult powers, with the provision of various charms, amulets, etc., professedly designed to keep the applicant or patient from the attention and power of demons, but actually to impress the applicant with the mysterious resources and powers of the sorcerer.

## SORCER

1. *magos* (μάγος, 3097), (a) "one of a Median caste, a magician": see wise; (b) "a wizard, sorcerer, a pretender to magic powers, a professor of the arts of witchcraft," Acts 13:6, 8, where Bar-Jesus was the Jewish name, Elymas, an Arabic word meaning "wise." Hence the name Magus, "the magician," originally applied to Persian priests. In the Sept., only in Dan. 2:2, 10, of the "enchanters," (KJV, "astrologers"), of Babylon.

## IMPOSTORS

Goes (γόης, 1114) primarily denotes "a wailer" (goao, "to wail"); hence, from the howl in which spells were chanted, "a wizard, sorcerer, enchanter," and hence, "a juggler, cheat, impostor," rendered "impostors" in 2 Tim. 3:13, (KJV), "seducers."

## WHISPERER, WHISPERING

1. *psithuristes* (ψιθυριστής, 5588), "a whisperer," occurs in an evil sense in Rom. 1:29.

2. *psithurismos* (ψιθυρισμός, 5587), "a whispering," is used of "secret slander" in 2 Cor. 12:20. In the Sept., Eccl. 10:11, of "a murmured enchantment." Note: Synonymous with No. 1 is katalalos, "a backbiter" (Rom. 1:30), the distinction being that this denotes one guilty of open calumny (slander), psithuristes, one who does it.[69]

## BEWITCH

1. baskaino (βασκαίνω, 940), primarily, "to slander, to prate about anyone"; then "to bring evil on a person by feigned (pretend) praise, or mislead by an evil eye, and so to charm, bewitch" (Eng., "fascinate" is connected), is used figuratively in Gal. 3:1, of leading into evil doctrine.

2. *existemi* (ἐξίστημι, 1839) is rendered "bewitch" in Acts 8:9, 11, KJV, concerning Simon the sorcerer; it does not mean "to bewitch," as in the case of the preceding verb, but "to confuse, amaze." [70]

As a means to keep men in bondage, diabolical spirits use their human agents to release havoc by the use of witchcraft, sorcery, and the like.

### Rebellious Angels Taught Mankind War

> Moreover Azazyel taught men to make swords, knives, shields, breastplates . . . so that the world became altered.   Book of Enoch 8:1 [71]

One fallen angel trained men to make weapons such as swords, knives, shields and breastplates" (Book of Enoch 8:1). I find it interesting the first polygamist, Lamech, took for himself two wives; "Adah meaning "beauty," and Zillah, "shade or tinkling" indicating darkness, the use of charms, and pointing to witchcraft.[72] Cain's family line was an open door for diabolical spirits. By the time we get to Lamech, he participated in the Nephilim deeds of multiple sex partners and violence. Lamech and Zillah conceived a son who became an instructor in metal craftsmanship including articles for war. Lamech himself acted like the Nephilim.

> Lamech said to his wives, "Adah and Zillah, listen to me; wives of Lamech, hear my words. I have killed a man for wounding me, a young man for injuring me. Genesis 4:23

Neiphilim seeded nations possessed with advanced weaponry were the first to produce and use chariots of iron. By design these chariots instilled fear in their enemies.

> ". . . though the Canaanites have iron chariots and though they are strong, you can drive them out." Joshua 17:18b

Azazyel was one of the fornicating "sons of God" in the Book of Enoch who taught men to make these articles of war. This is an indication Tubal-Cain was a recipient of this education.

> And Zillah, she also bare Tubalcain, an instructor of every artificer in brass and iron . . . Genesis 4:22 KJV

# Chapter 19

## Access to the Body

Now the body *is* not for fornication, but for the Lord; and the Lord for the body. 14And God hath both raised up the Lord, and will also raise up us by his own power. 15Know ye not that your bodies are the members of Christ? *shall I then take the members of Christ, and make them the members of an harlot? God forbid. 16What? know ye not that he which is joined to an harlot is one body? for two, saith he, shall be one flesh. 17But he that is joined unto the Lord is one spirit. 18Flee fornication. Every sin that a man doeth is without the body; but he that committeth fornication sinneth against his own body.* 19What? know ye not that your body is the temple of the Holy Ghost *which is* in you, which ye have of God, and ye are not your own?

20For ye are bought with a price: therefore glorify God in your body, and in your spirit, which are God's. 1Corinthians 6:13b-20

Nephilim spirits gain access to a human body through the door of sexual immorality. When two people join together in sex, they become one physically. Sexually immorality is a sin against your own body. In 1 Corinthians 6:16, the Greek word for "joined," kollaō, means "glue or fasten together" and refers to sexual contact with a harlot. Also used in 1 Corinthians 6:17 the same Greek word references the spiritual joining of a believer as "one" with the Lord.[73] A believer in Christ becomes a member or a part of the Lord's body and should never participate in immorality. By sexual contact, a physical and a spiritual joining occur. This is why Paul said in 1 Corinthians 6:15, "Never should a believer, male or female, join themselves to a prostitute or harlot!"

What we see in the natural world teaches us a spiritual reality (Romans 1:20). For instance, if one person carries a sexually transmitted disease, that disease infects their sex partner, and both people carry the disease. The same occurs in the spirit as well. Why do you think immorality is pushed as the okay thing to do? Because these spirits want access to oppress as many people as possible. They are vile, corrupt, unclean, and extremely nasty; through sexual immorality they have access. Some might think participating in sexual immorality has not harmed them, so let's look at what occurs because of it. Diseases are transmitted; unplanned pregnancies occur and may result in abortion causing death of an innocent child, and marriages are destroyed by infidelity, not considering the spiritual repercussions. What about the results of sexual immorality forced upon another, as rape and molestation, along with the psychological affects? Satanic forces seek to destroy and have been using sexual immorality to do so for centuries.

> And what agreement hath the temple of God with idols? for ye are the temple of the living God; as God hath said, I will dwell in them, and walk in [them]; and I will be their God, and they shall be my people. 2 Corinthians 6:16 KJ

A believer is one in spirit with the Lord, and if immoral with a prostitute, the spirit of prostitution gains a door to the body of Christ (the church) through the immorality of that person. A spirit of prostitution is a Nephilim spirit. The word for prostitute, pornē, means "a prostitute, a harlot, one who yields herself (or himself – my addition) to defilement for the sake of gain, any woman (or man- my addition) indulging in unlawful sexual intercourse, whether for gain or for lust, metaph. is an idolater."74 Think about our society today where sexual immorality is considered normal and expected. Is this much different in the church? Do you see how weakened the church has become just because of this one area of sin?

A spiritual mingling occurs through the door of the spiritual house provided by immorality. We see this principle in 1 Corinthians 7:14. If a believer is married to an unbeliever, the believer's spiritual union to the Lord sanctifies the marriage (makes it Holy). Why? children would be unclean without this occurring.

"For the unbelieving husband has been sanctified through his wife, and the unbelieving wife has been sanctified through her believing husband. Otherwise your children would be unclean, but as it is, they are holy (1 Corinthians 7:14).

The unbelieving spouse is sanctified because of his or her spouse's spiritual union with Christ. In a negative sense, evil spirits are unsanctified, and a spiritual union occurs through the sin of immoral sexual contact just as well.

> They joined themselves also unto Baalpeor, and ate the sacrifices to the dead. Psalms 106:28 KJ

Interestingly the word for "joined" in Psalms 106:28, *tsamad,* "to bind or fasten," carries the same meaning as "joined" in 1 Corinthians 6:16-17."[75] "They" in Psalms 106:28 refers to "Israel" as God's people. What did they do? "Joined...themselves to Baalpeor" and "the deity worshipped at Peor."[76]

Nephilim connect physical immorality with spiritual immorality as displayed by their religious practices. For example, Canaanite religious acts involved orgies, sex with shrine prostitutes, male or female, heterosexual or homosexual, to join themselves to the spirit they worshipped (2 Kings 23:7, 1 Kings 14:24, Hosea 4:14, Hosea 5:4). God told his people not to marry from Nephilim nations because they would become defiled.

> Do not intermarry with them. Do not give your daughters to their sons or take their daughters for your sons for they will turn your sons away from following me to serve other gods, and the LORD's anger will burn against you and will quickly destroy you. Deuteronomy 7:3-4

"Sons of God" forcefully and willfully thrust immorality into mankind and released a downward spiral toward complete degradation of society. Sexual immorality made the way for Satan to attack God's governing structures of family and church.

> 2Impiety increased; fornication multiplied; and they transgressed and corrupted all their ways. Book of Enoch 8:2 [77]

God set his governmental example for sexual relationship to exist between a man and his wife through Adam and Eve. Marriage symbolizes the union of God to his people, and its attack is spiritual.

> Marriage should be honored by all, and the marriage bed kept pure, for God will judge the adulterer and all the sexually immoral. Hebrews 13:4

Satan's seed adamantly oppose marriage as God designed. They promote sexual immorality of all kinds and lure many into sexual traps.

# Chapter 20

## Different Races of Giants

> 4The Nephilim were on the earth in those days—and also afterward... Genesis 6:4a

In the King James Bible over twenty references for Rephaim or giants exits.[78] Different sons of God bred with different women creating Nephilim variations. Rephaim were a race of giants defeated by Chedorlaomer and from them the Anakim, Zuzim, and Emim were believed to have descended (Genesis 14:5). King Og was a Rephaim progeny from Bashan who slept in a bed more than "thirteen feet long and six feet wide" (Deuteronomy 3:11 NLT).

> 1Hear, O Israel. You are now about to cross the Jordan to go in and dispossess nations greater and stronger than you, with large cities that have walls up to the sky. 2The people are strong and tall—Anakites! You know about them and have heard it said: "Who can stand up against the Anakites?" Deuteronomy 9:1-2

Anakites were another variation of Nephilim who descended from Anak. The giant Arba from Hebron fathered Anak whose descendants became a nomadic race of giants.[79] Some such as Zamzummims or Zuzims may be of the same or a different nationality (Duet. 2:20). Each race of giants would have differing cultures which would affect how they lived.

# Chapter 21

# God's Responds

> Yet the LORD warned Israel and Judah through all His prophets and every seer, saying, "Turn from your evil ways and keep My commandments, My statutes according to all the law which I commanded your fathers, and which I sent to you through My servants the prophets." 2 Kings 17:13 NASB

### He Sends a Man

Before judgment comes, God in his mercy sends a prophet to warn and cry out to whosoever will hear "Repent, then, and turn to God, so that your sins may be wiped out" (Acts 3:19). God found one man before the flood to do the job, and his name was Noah.

> But Noah found grace in the eyes of the Lord. Noah was a righteous man, blameless in his time; Noah walked with God" (Genesis 6:8-9b).

> The LORD then said to Noah, "Go into the ark, you and your whole family, because I have found you righteous in this generation. Genesis 7:1 KJV

> 9These are the generations of Noah: Noah was a just man and perfect in his generations, and Noah walked with God. 10 And Noah begat three sons, Shem, Ham, and Japheth. Genesis 6:8-10 KJV

God calls a man or woman to the office of a prophet and uses his or her life as a sign and symbol to a particular generation in which he or she lives and to subsequent generations. The actual life of the prophet demonstrates what God plans to do and his message through him or her (Isaiah 8:18). A prophet's name and its meaning also bears significance as a part of the sign God portrays through them. Noah's name means rest (Genesis 5:29).[80] Through Noah, his father hoped rest would be found from man's toilsome labor. Noah symbolized salvation through faith. He was a man who rejected sin and believed God's word given to him. Because of Noah's faith in God's promise, he and his family were saved from judgment.

12God saw how corrupt the earth had become, for all the people on earth had corrupted their ways. 13So God said to Noah, "I am going to put an end to all people, for *the earth is filled with violence because of them*. I am surely going to destroy both them and the earth. 14So make yourself an ark of cypress wood; make rooms in it and coat it with pitch inside and out. 17 I am going to bring floodwaters on the earth to destroy all life under the heavens, every creature that has the breath of life in it. Everything on earth will perish. 18But I will establish my covenant with you, and you will enter the ark—you and your sons and your wife and your sons' wives with you. 22Noah did everything just as God commanded him. Genesis 6:12-14; 17-18; 22

# Chapter 22

## Sin and Unclean Spirits

> For our struggle is not against flesh and blood, but against the rulers, against the powers, against the world forces of this darkness, against the spiritual forces of wickedness in the heavenly places. Ephesians 6:12 NASB

At this point in our study we need to be clear about the relationship between sin and evil spirits. Sin initially arose from Satan, an external spiritual force outside of man. Satan required access to the physical body of men to accomplish his vision for earth and went after Adam and Eve to get it. Other fallen spirits seek physical bodies as well. How do they acquire one? The same way Satan seized humanity: by tempting humans into sin.

> 8Be self-controlled and alert. Your enemy the devil prowls around like a roaring lion looking for someone to devour. 9Resist him, standing firm in the faith, because you know that your brothers throughout the world are undergoing the same kind of sufferings. 1 Peter 5:8-9

Nephilim and their seed provide Satan with a supply of people who live totally to gratify their sin nature and do not resist sin so fallen spirits can control earth through them. Sin occurs when a law of God is broken and thus brings the wrath of God against its doer. Easton's Bible Dictionary provides us a definition of sin.

A transgression of the law of God" (1 John 3:4; Rom. 4:15), in the inward state and habit of the soul, as well as in the outward conduct of the life, whether by omission or commission (Rom. 6:12-17; 7:5-24). It is "not a mere violation of the law of our constitution, nor of the system of things, but an offence against a personal lawgiver and moral governor who vindicates his law with penalties. The soul that sins justly deserves punishment, and calls down the righteous wrath of God. Hence sin carries with it two inalienable characters, (1) guilt and (2) pollution." The moral character of a man's actions is determined by the moral state of his heart. The disposition to sin, or the habit of the soul that leads to the sinful act, is itself also sin (Rom. 6:12-17; Gal. 5:17; James 1:14, 15).[81]

Everyone who sins breaks the law; in fact, sin is lawlessness. 1 John 3:4

12Therefore do not let sin reign in your mortal body so that you obey its evil desires. 13Do not offer the parts of your body to sin, as instruments of wickedness, but rather offer yourselves to God, as those who have been brought from death to life; and offer the parts of your body to him as instruments of righteousness. 14For sin shall not be your master, because you are not under law, but under grace. 15 What then? Shall we sin because we are not under law but under grace? By no means! 16Don't you know that when you offer yourselves to someone to obey him as slaves, you are slaves to the one whom you obey—whether you are slaves to sin, which leads to death, or to obedience, which leads to righteousness? 17But thanks be to God that, though you used to be slaves to sin, you wholeheartedly obeyed the form of teaching to which you were entrusted. Romans 6:12-17

From the Amplified Bible we see again the acts of the sinful nature.

19Now the doings (practices) of the flesh are clear (obvious): they are immorality, impurity, indecency, 20 idolatry, sorcery, enmity, strife, jealousy, anger (ill temper), selfishness, divisions dissensions), party spirit (factions, sects with peculiar opinions, heresies),

> ²¹ envy, drunkenness, carousing, and the like. I warn you beforehand, just as I did previously, that those who do such things shall not inherit the kingdom of God. Galatians 5:19-21 Amplified Bible

When Adam and Eve took the bait from Satan, they made a choice to disobey a command from God which set them up for judgment. Sin originates from two sources, temptation by evil spirits and from man's own desire for evil.

> ¹³When tempted, no one should say, "God is tempting me." For God cannot be tempted by evil, nor does he tempt anyone; ¹⁴ but each person is tempted when they are dragged away by their own evil desire and enticed. ¹⁵ Then, after desire has conceived, it gives birth to sin; and sin, when it is full-grown, gives birth to death. James 1:13-15

Satan's kingdom gets access to men who give it to him. Satan's kingdom gets access through sin. After the fall, people must open the door to their heart and invite the Lord in. This can only take place by true repentance of sins and asking his forgiveness before a relationship can occur.

> Here I am! I stand at the door and knock. If anyone hears my voice and opens the door, I will come in and eat with him, and he with me. Revelations 3:20

Access to those who walk after their sin nature does not pose any difficulty to diabolical spirits. Men just need to be tempted to sin. If they give in, a door opens for these spirits to have access their lives.

> 13When tempted, no one should say, "God is tempting me." For God cannot be tempted by evil, nor does he tempt anyone; 14but each one is tempted when, by his own evil desire, he is dragged away and enticed. 15Then, after desire has conceived, it gives birth to sin; and sin, when it is full-grown, gives birth to death. James 1:13-15

Diabolical spirits may have many inroads to a person's life. Through iniquity the same types of sins are repeated in family lines. Access to the next generation by the same evil spirits that plagued their parents occurs. These spirits include infirmities and disease, which also pass through family lines. Through sin Satan gets an open door to a man. He could not get a door into Jesus because Jesus gave no place to sin (Matthew 4:1-11).

> 14Therefore, since we have a great high priest who has gone through the heavens, Jesus the Son of God, let us hold firmly to the faith we profess. 15For we do not have a high priest who is unable to sympathize with our weaknesses, but we have one who has been tempted in every way, just as we are—yet was without sin. Hebrews 4:14-15

People succumb to temptation from evil spirits when their own evil desires agree with the temptation and gains hold by thoughts and imaginations, as Eve's lure to eat forbidden fruit. Such thoughts motivate man's sin nature into action to do what it wants. But once again, it was Satan, a supernatural evil spirit who began sin's process. Sin wants to master a person in any given area to gain control of man's soul and either keep or lure them away from God.

> The wrath of God is being revealed from heaven against all the godlessness and wickedness of men who suppress the truth by their wickedness, Romans 1:18

Recall what Adam Spears and Alan Kline taught us: demons are dead Nephilim from the time of the flood and devils are fallen angels. Jesus showed his disciples how to handle these spirits who recognized and interfered with him as he went along. We must understand that these spirits dwell on earth and cause immense problems for the living. Jesus defeated the works of the devil by his triumphant sinless life, sacrificial death on the cross, and his resurrection from the dead.

> I am the Living One; I was dead, and behold I am alive for ever and ever! And I hold the keys of death and Hades. Revelations 1:18

Diabolical spirits must submit to the name of Jesus, which carries his full authority and power.

> 8And being found in appearance as a man, he humbled himself and became obedient to death—even death on a cross! 9Therefore God exalted him to the highest place and *gave him the name that is above every name, 10 that at the name of Jesus every knee should bow, in heaven and on earth and under the earth,* 11and every tongue confess that Jesus Christ is Lord, to the glory of God the Father. Philippians 2:8-11

Jesus came and told his disciples, "I have been given all authority in heaven and on earth. Matthew 28:18 NLT

> 15 He said to them, "But who do you say that I am?" 16 Simon Peter answered, "You are the Christ, the Son of the living God." 17 And Jesus said to him, "Blessed are you, Simon Barjona, because flesh and blood did not reveal this to you, but My Father who is in heaven. 18 "I also say to you that you are Peter, and upon this rock I will build My church; and the gates of Hades will not overpower it. 19 "I will give you the keys of the kingdom of heaven; and whatever you bind on earth shall have been bound in heaven, and whatever you loose on earth shall have been loosed in heaven." Matthew 16:15-19

Christ Jesus authorizes his disciple's use of his power and authority against Satan's kingdom to cast out evil spirits and heal all forms of sickness and disease.

> And when he had called unto [him] his twelve disciples, he gave them power [against] unclean spirits, to cast them out, and to heal all manner of sickness and all manner of disease. Matthew 10:1 KJV

> For unclean spirits, crying with loud voice, came out of many that were possessed [with them]: and many taken with palsies, and that were lame, were healed. Acts 8:7 KJV

> When the unclean spirit is gone out of a man, he walketh through dry places, seeking rest; and finding none, he saith, I will return unto my house whence I came out. Luke 11:24 KJV

Demons "walk" earth and are sometimes called unclean, foul, or evil spirits but do not forget they are dead Nephilim. Unclean greek, *akathartos*, denotes "morally impure, unclean in thought and life, not clean in a ceremonial sense, contaminated with 'a wrong mix' and therefore unclean." [82] Nephilim spirits would certainly be of a wrong mix, and everything they were before the flood; they would be after the flood but without a physical body. Man took on the nature of Satan at the fall. A demon or devil releases their essence to the human they occupy. If the Nephilim was a tyrant while alive, it existed as a tyrannical demon within the spirit realm on earth after death. If sexually perverse while alive, then as a demon spirit it remains the same and entices the living to do the same perversions while it goes along for the sensation.

> 23Just at that time there was in their synagogue a man [who was in the power] of an unclean spirit; and now [immediately] he raised a deep and terrible cry from the depths of his throat, saying, 24What have You to do with us, Jesus of Nazareth? Have You come to destroy us? I know who You are--the Holy One of God! 25And Jesus rebuked him, saying, Hush up (be muzzled, gagged), and come out of him! 26And the unclean spirit, throwing the man into convulsions and screeching with a loud voice, came out of him. 27And they were all so amazed an almost terrified that they kept questioning and demanding one of another, saying, What is this? What new (fresh) teaching! With authority He gives orders even to the unclean spirits and they obey Him! Mark 1:23-27 Amplified Bible

"One man with an unclean spirit raised a deep and terrible cry from the depths of his throat and spoke to Jesus and said, 'Let us alone'" (Mark 1:23-24). An individual with more than one unclean spirit gave voice to a ruling spirit who spoke to Jesus.

Unclean spirits see, speak, hear, and seek their desires just as we do because they are part human and part evil spirit. Because of their mixed origins, we read they are condemned to the darkness of earth and know they are eternally damned (Matthew 8:29). Evil spirits do not want to be detected, and for the most part we are unaware of their presence. Notice when Jesus dealt with unclean spirits, he did not allow them to carry on conversations with him and made them shut their mouths. Unclean spirits will talk and voice their opinions. Jesus remained the one in charge of any conversation. As the one in authority, he commanded and told them what to do and they obeyed.

> 11And whenever those possessed by evil (unclean) spirits caught sight of him, the spirits would throw them to the ground in front of him shrieking, "You are the Son of God!" 12 But Jesus sternly commanded the spirits not to reveal who he was. Mark 3:11-12 NLT

As Christians, we do not carry on conversations with evil spirits. We gain any understanding needed of the spirit realm from the Bible, along with the Holy Spirit who teaches and leads us.

> But when he, the Spirit of truth, comes, he will guide you into all truth. He will not speak on his own; he will speak only what he hears, and he will tell you what is yet to come. John 16:14

Man must accept or resist the solicitation coming from the diabolical spirit world. A door provides an entry way, and humans can open or shut doors into their lives from the spirit realm.

> Here I am! I stand at the door and knock. If anyone hears my voice and opens the door, I will come in and eat with him, and he with me. Rev 3:20

Even the Lord knocks on the door of men's hearts. Demons and devils tempt from outside of a human, just as temptation to sin sat at the door of Cain's heart before he gave it access. Through prayer we can ask for God's intervention which gives him admittance to mankind's affairs. God does not force himself upon any one, but the person who seeks him will find him.

> 1So they arrived at the other side of the lake, in the region of the Gerasenes. 2When Jesus climbed out of the boat, a man possessed by an evil (unclean) spirit came out from a cemetery to meet him. 3This man lived among the burial caves and could no longer be restrained, evenwith a chain. No one was strong enough to subdue him.5Day and night he wandered among the burial caves and in the hills, howling and cutting himself with sharp stones.6When Jesus was still some distance away, the man saw him, ran to meet him, and bowed low before him. 7With a shriek, he screamed, "Why are you interfering with me, Jesus, Son of the Most High God? In the name of God, I beg you, don't torture me!" 8For Jesus had already said to the spirit, "Come out of the man, you evil spirit." 9Then Jesus demanded, "What is your name? "And he replied, "My name is Legion, because there are many of us inside this man." 10Then the evil spirits begged him again

and again not to send them to some distant place. 11There happened to be a large herd of pigs feeding on the hillside nearby. 12"Send us into those pigs," the spirits begged. "Let us enter them."13So Jesus gave them permission. The evil spirits came out of the man and entered the pigs, and the entire herd of about 2,000 pigs plunged down the steep hillside into the lake and drowned in the water.14The herdsmen fled to the nearby town and the surrounding countryside, spreading the news as they ran. People rushed out to see what had happened. 15A crowd soon gathered around Jesus, and they saw the man who had been possessed by the legion of demons. He was sitting there fully clothed and perfectly sane, and they were all afraid. Mark 5:1-15 NLT

Unclean spirits drive their host to lifestyles of misery and physically self-destructive behaviors, even to extreme violence (Matthew 8:28). In this man, unclean spirits were in the thousands and enabled him with supernatural strength.[83]

28And when he was come to the other side into the country of the Gergesenes, there met him two possessed with devils, coming out of the tombs, exceeding fierce, so that no man might pass by that way. Matthew 8:28 KJV

Spirits who occupied him did not want to leave the region. Maybe these spirits believed they could reenter him later (Matthew 5:10). Unclean spirits recognized Jesus and also others who walk in his authority (Acts 19:15). Demons and devils may come and go from a host's body, with human preference, but animals will do (Matthew 8:32). At the command of Jesus, these unclean spirits entered two thousand pigs with the same destructive force as in their previous host, but the pigs could not withstand the torment. When unclean spirits left the man, he gained his mind back. This man would be an example of one seeded by these unclean spirits.

> And as he was yet a coming, the devil threw him down, and tare [him]. And Jesus rebuked the unclean spirit, and healed the child, and delivered him again to his father. Luke 9:42 KJV

Devils, unclean spirits attack children as well as adults.

> 21Leaving that place, Jesus withdrew to the region of Tyre and Sidon. 22A Canaanite woman from that vicinity came to him, crying out, "Lord, Son of David, have mercy on me! My daughter is suffering terribly from demon possession."23Jesus did not answer a word. So his disciples came to him and urged him, "Send her away, for she keeps crying out after us." 24He answered, "I was sent only to the lost sheep of Israel." 25The woman came and knelt before him. "Lord, help me!" she said. 26He replied, "It is not right to take the children's bread and toss it to their dogs." 27"Yes, Lord," she said, "but even the dogs eat the

crumbs that fall from their masters' table." 28Then Jesus answered, "Woman, you have great faith! Your request is granted." And her daughter was healed from that very hour. Matthew 15:21-28

A Canaanite mother cried out to Jesus for help because her demon-possession daughter suffered due to evil spirits. Any person demon-possessed, along with their family, will greatly suffer because of the evil spirit's presence. Jesus kept silent, but the woman continued to cry out until he finally spoke, "It is not right to take the children's bread and toss it to their dogs" (Matthew 15:21). Why did Jesus answer her in this manner? Matthew's information that the mother was a Canaanite is an important factor here. A Canaanite comes from a nation mixed with Nephilim, and his use of the word "dog" provides what we need to know. Children are humans, and a dog is a beast (Nephilim are called beasts). The root word for dog in this passage, "kyōn, indicates "someone whose moral impurity will exclude them from the New Jerusalem."84 Someone morally contaminated or polluted indicates to me that she was of the Nephilim. But Jesus said she had great faith, but it did not lead her to salvation. Jesus knew her heart; she sought help for herself, then her daughter. She came with no interest in salvation, and Jesus knew it.

> He (Jesus) did not need man's testimony about man, for he knew what was in a man. John 2:25

> Outside are the dogs, those who practice magic arts, the sexually immoral, the murderers, the idolaters and everyone who loves and practices falsehood. Rev 22:15

Demon-possessed, *daimonizomai,* means "to be under the power of a demon or a devil." [85] Possess denotes, "to occupy in person; to have a just right to; to be master of; to own; to possess property." [86] Diabolical spirits impose their thoughts and desires upon their host. Just as the definition denotes, evil spirits believe their human host is their property.

> [43] "Now when the unclean spirit goes out of a man, it passes through waterless places seeking rest, and does not find *it*. [44] Then it says, 'I will return to my house from which I came'; and when it comes, it finds *it* unoccupied, swept, and put in order. [45] Then it goes and takes along with it seven other spirits more wicked than itself, and they go in and live there; and the last state of that man becomes worse than the first. That is the way it will also be with this evil generation." Matthew 12:43-45 NASB

Here in Matthew he shares what happens when an unclean spirit goes out of a person. The spirit does not find rest outside a living body (waterless and dry); it decides to return to *"my house* from which I came" (Matthew 12:44). The unclean spirit believed the person's body belonged to them. When the evil spirit left, human life obtained the chance to return to normal. But if the sin by which the spirit entered still exists, this cycle repeats. Jesus bore the penalty for sin for all mankind on the cross, and if there is no repentance, these spirits can come and go at will. Unrepentant sins keep the swinging door open. In Matthew above, the man did not fill his house with righteousness (God's word). Since this did not happen, the first unclean spirit gets seven spirits more evil than itself to live in the man as well. Jesus states a fact, "That is the way it will also be with this evil generation" (Matthew 12:45c).

Very plainly, evil spirits use the living as their own, as human lives worsen because of the presence of these unclean spirits. In every generation evil spirits oppress and oppress some more because people reject God. So we see, evil spirits and people go hand and hand.

> For the wages of sin is death, but the free gift of God is eternal life in Christ Jesus our Lord. Romans 6:23 NASB

Jesus defeated Satan by the cross and holds the only power able to stop sin and evil spirits. As his authorized agents, the Church walks in his authority on earth and as his army, they fight to establish the kingdom of God and to release men from Satan's bondage.

# Chapter 23

# Back to Noah

Noah chose to walk with God and rejected the corruption of the Nephilim. To bring fulfillment of the second Adam, God could not use Nephilim tainted seed. Only pure Adamic humans would work, so God would move through Noah. All three of Noah's sons joined in the family ministry of building the ark before the first rain. Noah's relationship with God trained his family in righteousness, as they lived among a violent, immoral, perverse, depraved, and corrupted people. They took it all in: their father's walk with God and the debased generation about them. Noah's children and grandchildren would make their own decisions on how they would live. Would they walk with God or allow thoughts and temptation to draw them to repeat the sins of the people who died by the flood?

> And spared not the old world, but saved Noah the eighth [person], a preacher of righteousness, bringing in the flood upon the world of the ungodly; 2 Peter 2:5 KJV

Noah and Enoch were preachers before the flood as the Holy Spirit pleaded with the generations, but the earth rejected their supplication. Beyond the flood out of the invisible world, devils and spirits of dead Nephilim (demons) sought bodies to house. The only ones available initially were Noah and his family. Noah's three sons provide a glimpse of the generations who would emerge beyond the flood. Shem, Ham, and Japheth demonstrate to us what they believed by what they did.

> ... I will show you my faith by what I do.
> James 2:18b

God made a statement which provides an indication of man's heart condition even after the flood. "The LORD smelled the pleasing aroma and said in his heart: 'Never again will I curse the ground because of man, even though every inclination of his heart is evil from childhood. And never again will I destroy all living creatures, as I have done' (Genesis 8:21). It does not sound much different than before the deluge. "The LORD saw how great man's wickedness on the earth had become, and that every inclination of the thoughts of his heart was only evil all the time (Genesis 6:5). Every inclination of man's heart was evil before and after the flood, so not much changed. Mankind stood as easy pickings for spirits of the Nephilim.

Ancient text provides a scenario of the problems unclean demons posed to Noah's family and the working of Satan among men.

> "And in the third week of this jubilee the unclean demons began to lead astray the children of the sons of Noah; and to make to err and destroy them. 2. And the sons of Noah came to Noah their father, and they told him concerning the demons which were, leading astray and blinding and slaying his sons' sons. 3. And he prayed before the Lord his God, and said: God of the spirits of all flesh, who hast shown mercy unto me, And hast saved me and my sons from the waters of the flood, And hast not caused me to perish as Thou didst the sons of perdition; For Thy grace hath been great towards me, And great hath been Thy mercy to my soul; Let Thy grace be lift up upon my sons, And let not wicked spirits rule over them Lest they should destroy them from the earth. 4. But do Thou bless me and my sons, that we may increase and multiply and replenish the earth. 5. And Thou knowest how Thy Watchers, the fathers of these spirits, acted in my day: and as for these spirits which are living, imprison them and hold them fast in the place of condemnation, and let them not bring destruction on the sons of thy servant, my God; for these are malignant, and created in order to destroy. 6. And let them not rule over the spirits of the living; for

Thou alone canst exercise dominion over them. And let them not have power over the sons of the righteous from henceforth and for evermore." 7. And the Lord our God bade us to bind all. 8. And the chief of the spirits, Mastêmâ (Satan), came and said: "Lord, Creator, let some of them remain before me, and let them hearken to my voice, and do all that I shall say unto them; for if some of them are not left to me, I shall not be able to execute the power of my will on the sons of men; for *these are for* corruption and leading astray before my judgment, for great is the wickedness of the sons of men." 9. And He said: "Let the tenth part of them remain before him, and let nine parts descend into the place of condemnation." 10. And one of us He commanded that we should teach Noah all their medicines; for He knew that they would not walk in uprightness, nor strive in righteousness. 11. And we did according to all His words: all the malignant evil ones we bound in the place of condemnation and a tenth part of them we left that they might be subject before Satan on the earth. 12. And we explained to Noah all the medicines of their diseases, together with their seductions, how he might heal them with herbs of the earth. 13. And Noah wrote down all things in a book as we instructed him concerning every kind of medicine. Thus the evil spirits were precluded from (hurting) the sons of Noah. 14. And he gave all that he had written to Shem, his eldest son; for he loved him exceedingly above all his sons."[87]

Through Noah's sons, the earth became repopulated. These men revealed their character on an occasion when Noah drank too much wine.

> [18] And the sons of Noah, that went forth of the ark, were Shem, and Ham, and Japheth: and Ham is the father of Canaan. [19] These are the three sons of Noah: and of them was the whole earth overspread. [20] And Noah began to be an husbandman, and he planted a vineyard: [21] And he drank of the wine, and was drunken; and he was uncovered within his tent. [22] And Ham, the father of Canaan, saw the nakedness of his father, and told his two brethren without. [23] And Shem and Japheth took a garment, and laid it upon both their shoulders, and went backward, and covered the nakedness of their father; and their faces were backward, and they saw not their father's nakedness. [24] And Noah awoke from his wine, and knew what his younger son had done unto him. [25] And he said, Cursed be Canaan; a servant of servants shall he be unto his brethren. [26] And he said, Blessed be the LORD God of Shem; and Canaan shall be his servant. [27] God shall enlarge Japheth, and he shall dwell in the tents of Shem; and Canaan shall be his servant. Genesis 9:18-27 KJV

A drunk and naked Noah lay inside his tent when his son Ham entered and "saw" his father's nakedness. Saw, *ra'ah* means, "to see, look at, inspect, perceive, consider," as Ham not only stared but checked out his Father's nakedness.[88] Noah's genitals were most likely uncovered and Ham looked with no shame and maybe even in lust.

> But I tell you that anyone who looks at a woman lustfully has already committed adultery with her in his heart. Matthew 5:28

Next, Ham went out and made known his father's predicament to his brothers. Shem and Japheth took a garment and went into their father's tent backward to cover their father's nakedness without a stare. This was righteous behavior; Ham's behavior was unrighteous as he disrespected and humiliated his father.

> "Cursed is the man who dishonors his father or his mother." Then all the people shall say, "Amen!" Deuteronomy 27:16

Leviticus 18:6-7 helps us to understand the term to "uncover nakedness," which refers to sexual activity including intercourse. The NIV, NASB, and KJV translations together make this point clearer. In Leviticus Chapter 18, God told his children to avoid incestuous relationships.

Incest obviously was a Nephilim practice. Noah knew it and so did his sons including Ham and his grandson, Canaan (Leviticus 18:3).

> "None of you shall approach any blood relative of his to uncover nakedness; I am the LORD.' You shall not uncover the nakedness of your father, that is, the nakedness of your mother. She is your mother; you are not to uncover her nakedness." Leviticus 18:6-7 NASB

> "No one is to approach any close relative to have sexual relations. I am the LORD. 'Do not dishonor your father by having sexual relations with your mother. She is your mother; do not have relations with her. Leviticus 18:6-7

> The nakedness of your father, or the nakedness of your mother, shall you not uncover: she is your mother; you shall not uncover her nakedness. The nakedness of your father's wife shall you not uncover: it is your father's nakedness. Leviticus 18:7 KJV

These translations provide another possibility as the King James Bible indicates, "The nakedness of your father's wife shall you not uncover: it is your father's nakedness." Ham took advantage of the drunken state of his father and either observed or did some other inappropriate sexual behavior towards Noah, his wife, or both. It could have been possible that Noah's wife conceived sometime along the way and produced Canaan because Ham obviously displayed perverse sexual behavior toward others. This would help explain a specific repeated comment that Ham was the father of Canaan. This clarification would be given to indicate Ham and not Noah was the father of Canaan. Whatever took place; Ham yielded to sexual perversion and sinned.

> "Ham, the father of Canaan, saw his father's nakedness and told his two brothers outside. Genesis 9:22
>
> The sons of Noah who came out of the ark were Shem, Ham and Japheth. (*Ham was the father of Canaan.*) Genesis 9:18

Shem and Japheth honored their father, Ham did not. Noah's reaction the next morning, as a prophet of God, he spoke.

> 24 When Noah awoke from his wine, he knew what his youngest son had done to him. 25 So he said, "Cursed be Canaan; A servant of servants He shall be to his brothers." 26 He also said, "Blessed be the LORD, The God of Shem; And let Canaan be his servant. 27 "May God enlarge Japheth, And let him dwell in the tents of Shem; And let Canaan be his servant." 28 Noah lived three hundred and fifty years after the flood. 29 So all the days of Noah were nine hundred and fifty years, and he died. Genesis 9:24-28 KJV

Whatever Ham "did" to his father, Noah knew it.

> And Noah awoke from his wine, and knew what his younger son had done unto him. Genesis 9:24 KJV

Noah knew sexual perversion seized Ham in the same manner as pre-flood giants, and he may have seen the same in his grandson Canaan and pronounced it as such. Noah had enough of such sins, and here it came through his own family. Sin always has a payday whether recognized or not, "for the wages of sin is death" (Romans 6:23).

Sexual perversion brings a consequence and opens the door to Nephilim spirits. Cursed is Ham's son because of bondage to sin that Noah saw in Ham and in Canaan. The consequence of sin brought death and resulted in bondage. The sin nature was alive, and fallen spirits of the giants made their entrance through sexual perversion, the same way "sons of God" gained access to mankind before the flood and now afterwards. Noah prophesied that Canaan would be a slave to slaves, which indicated a double layer of bondage. Canaanites descendants were in bondage to Nephilim spirits of immorality and perversions, both sexual and spiritual.

Satan and his seed, the Nephilim, came to seize control of earth to enslave mankind. Idolatry and worship of devils and demons brings spiritual bondage, while sexual sins tie the body to these evil spirits.

> "I am the LORD your God, who brought you out of Egypt, out of the land of slavery. Exodus 20:2

Maybe we see God's anger because he delivered mankind from the Nephilim and all their wickedness by the flood. Here Ham opens the door by sexual perversion for these spirits to pollute mankind again. God cleansed the earth, but Ham opened the door for these spirits to operate again which exposed a heart of rebellion against God and his divine order.

# Chapter 24

# Judgment

> But they mocked God's messengers, despised his words and scoffed at his prophets until the wrath of the LORD was aroused against his people and there was no remedy. 2 Chronicles 36:16 NIV

Sinful man possesses the same propensity of depravity held by his or her previous generation as each generation adds more sin to the iniquity which requires a response from God. A judge reviews legal evidence in order to pass a verdict, and God is the ultimate judge. He passed judgment on the pre-flood generations (Genesis 6:5-6). At first judgment occurs to turn people from sin. If they do not pay attention and continue in sin, their hearts harden to the point of no remedy because they ignore the mercy of God.

> A man who remains stiff-necked after many rebukes will suddenly be destroyed--without remedy. Proverbs 29:1 NIV

When sins of a person or a nation become full, destruction comes. By the third and fourth generation of people who yoke themselves to sin, a level of wickedness emerges requiring a response from heaven.

But in the fourth generation they shall come here again: for the iniquity of the Amorites is not yet complete. Genesis 15:16 KJV

I believe those who carry a higher degree of Nephilim genetics also bear the same Nephilim disposition as in Biblical accounts. Due to the open door provided by sin, the same spirits continue to house a family line through its generations. Devils and demons manipulate to get people together for sexual contact and yoke people together who carry Nephilim genetics in their family lines. These breeders, led by evil spirits to other seeded people and their offspring, become stronger in Nephilim traits. We read where an evil spirit goes and gets other evil spirits more wicked than itself, indicating evil spirit works the spirit realm to bring greater degrees of evil into the lives of people (Matthew 12:45). Sin, greater degrees of wickedness, genetics, along with lifestyles of immorality continue to breed Nephilim seed. All the while they become more wicked and stronger in manifestation. By the third and fourth generation in Nephilim family lines, we find full blown Nephilim in behavior and sin. If not dealt with, seed of Nephilim will tolerate only a few and seek to kill or enslave the rest. God sends judgment to cleanse the earth of them so others can survive.

> 'The LORD is slow to anger and abounding in steadfast love, forgiving iniquity and transgression, but he will by no means clear the guilty, visiting the iniquity of the fathers on the children, to the third and the fourth generation.' Numbers 14:18 ESV

> Keeping mercy for thousands, forgiving iniquity and transgression and sin, and that will by no means clear the guilty; visiting the iniquity of the fathers upon the children, and upon the children's children, unto the third and to the fourth generation. Exodus 34:7 KJ

In Exodus 34:7, the iniquity of the fathers transfers to their children unto the third and fourth generations. Since Ham opened the door, we'll see what occurred through a family line oppressed with spirits of the Nephilim. Ham's lineage through Canaan finds those under a curse who epitomize captivity to sin.

A curse transfers due to sin. A good example occurs in 2 Kings 5. Elisha the prophet refused to take any gifts from Naaman after his restoration from leprosy. Gehazi (Elisha's servant) went after the gifts and lied about it. The curse of Naaman's leprosy came upon Gehazi and his family line. Sin in Ghazis' case resulted in a physical disease.

> 26 But Elisha asked him, "Don't you realize that I was there in spirit when Naaman stepped down from his chariot to meet you? Is this the time to receive money and clothing, olive groves and vineyards, sheep and cattle, and male and female servants? 27 Because you have done this, you and your descendants will suffer from Naaman's leprosy forever." When Gehazi left the room, he was covered with leprosy; his skin was white as snow. 2 Kings: 26-27 NLT

Adam, Eve, and Cain all received curses upon themselves and their family lines.

> To Adam he said, "Because you listened to your wife and ate from the tree about which I commanded you, 'You must not eat of it,' "Cursed is the ground because of you; through painful toil you will eat of it all the days of your life. 19 By the sweat of your brow you will eat your food until you return to the ground, since from it you were taken; for dust you are and to dust you will return." Genesis 3:17, 19

> 16To the woman he said, "I will greatly increase your pains in childbearing; with pain you will give birth to children. Your desire will be for your husband, and he will rule over you." Genesis 3:16

> Now you (Cain)* are under a curse and driven from the ground, which opened its mouth to receive your brother's blood from your hand. Genesis 4:11 *(My Addition)

A curse not only affects the life of a sinner, but the land came under a curse as well because of Adam's sin. It became harder for him to produce from the soil. Eve received a curse of increased pain in childbirth, and Cain became a wander. Canaan's sin was of a sexual nature and resulted in homosexuality in his seed. Sin produces a curse, and it affects the life of the person and their descendants and brings bondage in some form or another. Bondage comes out of the Nephilim whose rebellion against God's laws results in curses.

The Promised Land, also called Canaan Land, was full of Nephilim nations. Egypt is called the land of Ham in Psalms 105:23, and the land from which God delivered his people from slavery.

> Then he cursed Canaan, the son of Ham: "May Canaan be cursed! May he be the lowest of servants to his relatives." Genesis 9:25 NLT

# Chapter 25

# Mighty Men

> 20And again he said, Where unto shall I liken the kingdom of God? It is like leaven, which a woman took and hid in three measures of meal, till the whole was leavened. Luke 13:20-21 KJV

Three times Satan sewed his yeast of destruction into mankind; in the garden with Adam and Eve causing their fall, and by the sons of God before and after the flood.

In the parable of the leaven bread, Nephilim children cannot be distinguished once mixed into Adam's seed and this leaven sewn three times totally permeates mankind. *Leaven in Greek, "zymē, denotes of chronic mental and moral corruption, viewed in its tendency to infect others."*[89] This is a most accurate description of Nephilim poison and its ability to spread.

The sins and spirits of the Nephilim locked onto Ham and his descendants. By the fourth generation from Noah, third from Ham, we see the term "mighty men" occur again.

> There were giants in the earth *in those days; and also after that*, when the sons of God came in unto the daughters of men, and they bore children to them, the same became *mighty men* (strongs #1368 gibbor) which were of old, men of renown. Genesis 6:4 KJV

Out of the lineage of Ham comes the first one to be identified as a "mighty one" (*gibbor*) beyond the flood. When sons of God came to sew their destruction back into Adam's seed, Ham's descendants provided easy targets because the sins of their father (sexual immorality and perversion) that followed them.

> 6 The sons of Ham: Cush, Egypt, Put, and Canaan. 7 The sons of Cush: Seba, Havilah, Sabtah, Raamah, and Sabteca. The sons of Raamah: Sheba and Dedan. 8 Cush fathered Nimrod; he was the first on earth to be a mighty man. 9 He was a mighty hunter before the LORD. Therefore it is said, "Like Nimrod a mighty hunter before the LORD." Genesis 10:6-9 ESV

Post flood produces the first *gibbor* and speaks of Nimrod, a despot (tyrant, dictator), in the earth.

> 9He was a *mighty* (strongs #1368 gibbor) hunter before the LORD: wherefore it is said, Even as Nimrod the *mighty* (strongs #1368 gibbor) hunter before the LORD. 10And the beginning of his kingdom was Babel, and Erech, and Accad, and Calneh, in the land of Shinar. Genesis 10:9-10 KJV

Notice a "mighty one" seeks power to rule or dominates over others and exalt themselves as a god. Nimrod became a tyrannical head of government who took in more territory in acquisition of power. Tyrannical government leaders all around the world oppress and shed innocent blood without concern. We must understand Nephilim spirits manifest themselves as terrorists, bullies, gang members, drug lords, con artists and also through any organized crime and the like. At the root of organized crime lies distribution of prostitution and illegal drugs, which go right back to corruption from Nephilim, which goes straight back to rebellious angels, then to Satan himself. Tyranny originated from Satan and through Nephilim spirits; these cycles repeat throughout time. Wherever corruption exists, behind the scenes you'll find people motivated by Nephilim spirits.

> 11 Now the whole earth had one language and the same words. ² And as people migrated from the east, they found a plain in the land of Shinar and settled there. ³ And they said to one another, "Come, let us make bricks, and burn them thoroughly." And they had brick for stone, and bitumen for mortar. ⁴ Then they said, "Come, let us build ourselves a city and a tower with its top in the heavens, and let us make a name for ourselves, lest we be dispersed over the face of the whole earth." ⁵ And the Lord came down to see the city and the tower, which the children of man had built. ⁶ And the Lord said, "Behold, they are one people, and they have all one language, and this is only the beginning of what they will do. And

nothing that they propose to do will now be impossible for them. ⁷ Come, let us go down and there confuse their language, so that they may not understand one another's speech." ⁸ So the LORD dispersed them from there over the face of all the earth, and they left off building the city. Genesis 11:1-8 ESV

A "tower that reaches to the heavens" sounds like a Nephilim inspired building project. They gathered together, built a city, a pagan worship center (within the tower), and a name for themselves. In gathering together they were breeding and increasing their seed. Everything they sought was in rebellion against God. God had to slow them down or earth would have quickly become as before the flood.

Nimrod's name in itself means rebellion which is the sin of witchcraft which typifies the Nephilim. Witchcraft yields interference from the kingdom of darkness, and Nimrod and family obviously used it.

> For rebellion [is as] the sin of witchcraft and stubbornness [is as] iniquity and idolatry. 1 Samuel 15:23a KJV

Nimrod gathered men about him of Nephilim mindsets. By this time I am sure demons and devils had themselves plenty of human houses, and they raised their fists against heaven. Spirits of the Nephilim used the men of that day to voice their anger at God, probably for his prior judgment against them by the flood. God put a stop to a one world order under this Nephilim. He sent confusion of languages to remove this threat against his plan to send our Redeemer."[90]

# Chapter 26

# Mingled Seed

God created all seed-bearing plants and trees bearing fruit with seed to reproduce according to its own kind. The same holds true of all creatures of the sea, earth, fowls of the air, as well as mankind. The species were not to inter- breed keeping corruption out and purity in.

> Ye shall keep my statutes. Thou shalt not let thy cattle gender with a diverse kind: thou shalt not sow thy field with mingled seed: neither shall a garment mingled of linen and woolen come upon thee. Lev 19:19 KJ

In the book of Enoch, we can see the extent that corruption and violence laid claim to life on earth due to the Nephilim.

> And when men could no longer sustain them (the giants), 4. The giants turned against them and devoured mankind. 5.And they began to sin against birds, and beasts, and reptiles, and fish, and to

> devour one another's flesh, and drink the blood. 6. Then the earth laid accusation against the lawless. Book of Enoch Chapter 7:4-6 [91]

> And there arose much godlessness, and they committed fornication, and they were led astray, and became corrupt in all their ways. Book of Enoch, Chapter 8:2

Sons of God posed as counterfeits of human men, something they were not and produced offspring with the same character traits as natural pretenders. Twice dead in their spirits and souls, mingled seeded humans live totally to satisfy their sin nature. God gave instructions to Israel to prevent mingling with Nephilim nations. Why? If disobeyed they would breed Nephilim genetics into their normal population and take Nephilim spiritual and immoral practices as their own.

> Instead, they mingled among the pagans and adopted their evil customs. Psalm 106:35 NLT

The end results of one male breeder with multiple female sex partners can be mind boggling. Historical figures Moulay Ismaïl Ibn Sharif and Genghis Khan were two oppressive, tyrannical leaders whose procreation must have rived their need for water. Sharifian Emperor of Morocco (1672-1727) fathered 1,000 plus offspring with over 800 live births.[92] Along with his wives, he kept a harem of 500 captive women available to him for sex.[93] Creator of the Mongol empire (1162–1227),

Genghis Khan's Y chromosome continues an invasion into modern times. Mr. Khan can call "16 million or approximately 1 out of 200 living males, his direct descendants." ₉₄, ₉₅ ₀This feat and practice of one male makes the Nephilim breeding strategy clear.

If a person participates in sex with someone infected with a Nephilim spirit or carries the genetics of Nephilim, the Nephilim spirit transfers and the genes may also if conception takes place. God's people did not listen and became just like the Nephilim nations.

> ⁶ and they intermarried with them. Israelite sons married their daughters, and Israelite daughters were given in marriage to their sons. Judges 3:6 NLT

> ¹¹But listen carefully to everything I command you today. Then I will go ahead of you and drive out the Amorites, Canaanites, Hittites, Perizzites, Hivites, and Jebusites. ¹² "Be very careful never to make a treaty with the people who live in the land where you are going. If you do, you will follow their evil ways and be trapped. ¹³ Instead, you must break down their pagan altars, smash their sacred pillars, and cut down their Asherah poles. ¹⁴ You must worship no other gods, for the LORD, whose very name is Jealous, is a God who is jealous about his relationship with you. ¹⁵ "You must not make a treaty of any kind with the people living in the land. They lust after their gods, offering sacrifices to them. They will invite you to join them in their sacrificial meals, and you will go with them. ¹⁶ Then you will accept their daughters, who sacrifice to other gods, as wives for your sons. And they will seduce your sons to commit adultery against me by

worshiping other gods. Exodus 34:11-16 NLT

Scripture states so well Satan's achievement by means of the Nephilim. They lead many in each generation in their ways. Satan successfully mingled the seed of the Nephilim with humans, but God always preserves for himself a remnant for himself within each generation.

> The people of Israel, and the priests and the Levites, have not separated themselves from the peoples of the lands, doing according to their abominations, even of the Canaanites, the Hittites, the Perizzites, the Jebusites, the Ammonites, the Moabites, the Egyptians, and the Amorites. 2For they have taken of their daughters for themselves and for their sons, *so that the holy seed have mingled themselves with the peoples of the lands:* yea, the hand of the princes and rulers hath been chief in this trespass. Ezra 9:1a-2 ASV

# Chapter 27

## Neanderthals and the Nephilim

> 33 Do not be deceived: "Bad company corrupts good morals." 1 Corinthians 15:33 NASB

While writing this book, advancement in DNA technology confirmed different species of humans did indeed interbred and intermingled their genes.[96] Evidence of interbreeding between humans and Neanderthals became obvious over sixty years ago from ancient bones discovered in a Romanian cave. [97]

Moses informed us in Genesis 6:4 that the Nephilim were a crossbreed and now this has been physically confirmed. To be clear, modern terms such as Neanderthals and Denisovans are really just different species of Biblical Nephilim. [98] Exactly what percentage of Neanderthal DNA exists in modern humans are not known for sure, but it's there. [99]

> "Now God saw that the earth had become corrupt and was filled with violence." Genesis 6:11 NLT

The Book of Enoch informs us of different factions of Nephilim that devoured one another, and with evidence of cannibalism, they literally did.

> 22 And they begat sons the Naphidim, and they were all unlike, and they devoured one another: and the Giants slew the Naphil, and the Naphil slew the Eljo, and the Eljo mankind, and one man another. Book of Jubilees 7:22-23[100]

> 10Restore the earth, which the angels have corrupted; and announce life to it, that I may revive it. 11All the sons of men shall not perish in consequence of every secret, by which the Watchers have destroyed, and *which* they have taught, their offspring.12All the earth has been corrupted by the effects of the teaching of Azazyel. To him therefore ascribe the whole crime.13To Gabriel also the Lord said, Go to the biters, to the reprobates, to the children of fornication; and destroy the children of fornication, the offspring of the Watchers, from among men; bring them forth, and excite them one against another. Let them perish by *mutual* slaughter; for length of days shall not be theirs. Book of Enoch, Chapter 10:10-13[101]

A few articles on the Neanderthals allow us to ratify more evidence of Biblical accounts of the Nephilim.

Article 1

*The Wickedness of the Pre-Flood World.* Written by: Arnold C. Mendez, Sr. (This is the conclusion of this article.)

> The fossil record of early man supports what the book of Genesis indicates. During this time period cannibalism was common. The wholesale slaughter and murder of men is expressed in the cast off fossil remnants laying on the trash heap of many an excavated site. The bones of fellow human beings were butchered, cut apart, and then cast into garbage pits where they mixed with rotting pig, elephant, and wolf carcasses. The skeletal remains of the fossil record shows that *H. erectus*, *H. neanderthalensis*, and *H. sapiens* were living in violent societies.[102]

One of the saddest details in Mr. Mendez's article was the excavation of what probably had been an entire family: mom, dad, and children, butchered and eaten at the dining pleasure of their cold hearted capturers. [103]

Article 2

Stan Gooch & the Neanderthal Legacy Published in New Dawn Magazine, New Dawn No. 125 (Mar-Apr 2011). Written by Oana R. Ghiocel, M.A. & Robert M. Schoch, Ph.D.

"Stan Gooch, a psychologist and linguist extensively studied and wrote several books on the Neanderthals. He passed away in 2010."[104]

Stan Gooch's view; modern humanity is a result of the intermixing, both biologically and culturally, of Cro-Magnon and Neanderthal elements. Neanderthal culture, more sophisticated than that of the Cro-Magnons when they first arrived in Europe, served as a primary source for much so- called ancient wisdom.

Gooch argued that Neanderthals were the original creators, the innovators, of high culture, of symbolic values and religious sensibilities, which early modern humans (Cro-Magnons) copied and adopted without genuine understanding. Neanderthal culture was not a civilization of high technologies, but one of the mind and spirit that survives today in our beliefs, myths, folklore, and religious practices.

Neanderthals, according to Gooch, worshipped the cave bear, the spider, and the serpent – animals with whom they shared their caves. Neanderthals were the first humans to fully develop religious cults, and cave bear worship was their most significant cult. Neanderthals worshipped the number 13, associated with the moon and the lunar calendar, a number that is still considered magical today. Neanderthals developed a profound knowledge of crystals and minerals. According to Gooch, Neanderthals developed their own unique symbols, signs, and sophisticated language systems. Neanderthals weaved and sewed embroidery, wore jewelry, painted their faces and bodies, danced, had an elaborate mythology and cosmology, built stone circles, utilized sacred fires, and made ceremonial sacrifices. They had their own grand celebrations and feasts, which were spectacularly colorful and creative performances.

They worshipped the moon and other celestial bodies including constellations still worshipped today worldwide such as The Big Bear, Little Bear, and Draco (the dragon or serpent in the sky). Gooch asserted that Neanderthals had a strong religious life, based on an earth-magic religion, and they believed in the afterlife, practicing complex burial rituals.

I believe the actuality of Neanderthal man – of whom archaeologists find only a handful of skeletons, a few altars, traces of ritualized burial, a range of flint tools, and an apparent knowledge of herbal remedies – was this: his was a moon-goddess-worshipping, matriarchal, food-gathering society, where women governed all matters. The only tasks delegated specifically to men were those where muscle power was directly and literally required, as in fighting, for example. The structure and nature of Cro-Magnon life was diametrically opposite. This was a patriarchal, hunter- warrior society, of which men governed all aspects, including religious life. Women were mere adjuncts in all things, whose main purpose was to bear sons and to comfort and care for the male. The supreme deity worshipped was the sun god.

## The Cerebrum and Cerebellum

The vertebrate brain includes the cerebrum and the cerebellum. In modern humans the cerebrum consists of the cerebral hemispheres that fill most of the skull. In humans the cerebellum is smaller than the cerebrum and situated at the back of the head tucked behind and under the cerebrum. The cerebrum is associated with "logical" and "rational" thinking, versus the cerebellum is associated with "dreaming" and "magic."

The cerebellum… is responsible for trance states, for dreams, for telepathy, for psychic healing, for spontaneous wounds, for poltergeist phenomena, and *all* other such matters. It is also the source of and the impetus for religious belief. The Neanderthal brain had a much larger and more powerful cerebellum than that found in Cro-Magnons. The more developed Neanderthal cerebellum gave rise to their "high civilization of dreams

Gooch believed there were several different varieties of Neanderthals, separated geographically and temporally, in Europe, Africa, the Middle East, and Asia. Furthermore, a key point of his thesis is that Neanderthals, at least some Neanderthals, could and did interbreed with our direct ancestors, the Cro-Magnons. Gooch believed that aggressive and battle-skilled Cro-Magnons both massively exterminated some populations of Neanderthals and also interbred with them. The genetic crossing of Cro-Magnon and

Neanderthal produced not just (a) highly gifted individuals ('the mighty men of old, the men of renown') but (b) an entirely new species of human – ourselves…. This new product was either entirely or very largely due to Cro-Magnon men fertilizing Neanderthal women – not the other way around.

These offspring would have been accepted into Cro-Magnon groups.... And so Neanderthal genes were introduced into the Cro-Magnon gene pool" [105]

Neanderthals first organized religious cults around idolatry and the worship of creation, which God forbad (Exodus 20:1-4). Mr. Gooch believed the Neanderthals were originators of the religion they practiced, and I would have to agree. I believe the beginning of structured idolatry and false worship came from the Nephilim. The conception of "mother nature" and "mother earth" worship originated from the Neanderthals as well. This makes perfect sense as Neanderthal matriarchal rulers exalted and worshipped a god in the form of a female (moon goddess).

Neanderthal culture furthermore evolved around the use of psychoactive drugs which induced hallucinate states. Such a condition was used in worship and contact with the spirit world. Cave drawings of ancient shamans smoking long pipes confirmed such practices.[106] The Book of Enoch stated the uses of these types of drugs were taught to their offspring by fallen angels.

Neanderthal interbreeding with Cro-Magnon began in the Middle East region and branched out, just as the Book of Enoch indicates. Since violence was a prevalent part of their culture, sexual contact would have consisted of rape, as well as consensual sex.

Researchers also believe Neanderthals and humans interbred to the point Neanderthals became indistinguishable with any other human (Chapter 17 Blending In).[107] Recall sons of god rebelled and used sex for their purposes. Nephilim use sexual seduction to ensnare a victim, and this character trait links to both males and females. Canaanite women would dress in garments of a prostitute and wait for a sex partner, engage in their immorality, and go on their way. The story of Tamar, who played a shrine prostitute in order to conceive, gives us an idea of what went on (Genesis 38:15-21).

> [15]Judah noticed her and thought she was a prostitute, since she had covered her face. [16] So he stopped and propositioned her. "Let me have sex with you," he said, not realizing that she was his own daughter-in-law. [21] So he asked the men who lived there, "Where can I find the shrine prostitute who was sitting beside the road at the entrance to Enaim?" Genesis 38:15; 21 NLT

It also seems Cro-Magnon (Adam's seed) were drawn to the Neanderthal's culture and pagan religion, just as Israel was drawn to the Nephilim nations in the Canaan land. Males knew of sexual opportunities and even orgies in the Nephilim communities, so many came. Mr. Gooch indicates Cro-Magnon did a lot of breeding with Neanderthal women. These women knew how to use witchcraft, manipulation and seduction to lure men into their sexual traps.

> 1My son, pay attention to my wisdom; listen carefully to my wise counsel. 2Then you will show discernment, and your lips will express what you've learned. 3For the lips of an immoral woman are as sweet as honey, and her mouth is smoother than oil. 4But in the end she is as bitter as

poison, as dangerous as a double-edged sword. 5Her feet go down to death; her steps lead straight to the grave. 6 For she cares nothing about the path to life. She staggers down a crooked trail and doesn't realize it. Proverbs 5:1-6 NLT

Pagan religious practices of Neanderthals such as "witchcraft, charms, enchantments, cutting of roots, sorcery, astrology, divination, acquainting them with plants and signs, use of crystals for fortune telling, and idolatry also confirms information from the Book of Enoch (Book of Enoch 7:1).

I believe in Mr. Gooch's studies we find the origins of feminism. Neanderthals women governed all aspects of life and delegated duties to their men that surrounded physical strength and their ability to fight. Mr. Gooch tells us Cro-Magnon's culture was the complete opposite, where warrior males governed their society and women provided supportive roles for their husbands and children.

Satan used the Neanderthals/Nephilim to sow chaos into all aspects of human life (Genesis 6). When given opportunity these spirits seek positions of power through their human hosts, including the opposite sex. A conflict of female verses male arose out of the merger of Neanderthals and Cro-Magnon cultures. How do I know? This conflict between the sexes continues today and naturally would have developed when their cultures combined. There is a flow of authority in the kingdom of God, and those who submit will enjoy its benefit. Forced dominance for whatever reason raises anger and division. This comes from the evil one and not from God.

According to Mr. Gooch the Neanderthals believed they were the enlightened ones; this came because of their origins and their natural allurement and interaction with evil spirits (who exalt themselves). Nephilim seed are drawn to Satan and occultist practices because these spirits move through their family lines and naturally draw them. Mr. Gooch also told us the Neanderthal's cerebellum was larger than normal human brains. This would facilitate interaction with the unseen world and probably genetically acquired from their angelic fathers.

Demonic forces gained access through every one of these modes of Nephilim corruption as Mr. Gooch taught. The whole point of the Nephilim was to create seed for Satan. They had to blend into mankind and the only way that occurred was by sexual intercourse with the rapid method of multiple partners.

I will leave this chapter with a section from *Wisdom of Solomom,* a book *written* around one hundred years prior to Christ coming to earth. An unnamed writer, well versed in scripture, wrote at a time of oppression and great difficulty.

> "3For truly, the ancient inhabitants of your holy land, 4 whom you hated for deeds most odious—Works of witchcraft and impious sacrifices; 5 a cannibal feast of human flesh and of blood, from the midst of...— These merciless murderers of children, 6 and parents who took with their own hands defenseless lives, You willed to destroy by the hands of our fathers, 7 that the land that is dearest of all to you might receive a worthy colony of

God's children. 8But even these, as they were men, you spared, and sent wasps as forerunners of your army that they might exterminate them by degrees. 9 Not that you were without power to have the wicked vanquished in battle by the just, or wiped out at once by terrible beasts or by one decisive word; 10 But condemning them bit by bit, you gave them space for repentance. *You were not unaware that their race was wicked and their malice ingrained, and that their dispositions would never change; 11for they were a race accursed from the beginning.* Neither out of fear for anyone did you grant amnesty for their sins. Wisdom of Solomon 12:3-10 [108]

# Chapter 28

# Mindsets

> The LORD observed the extent of human wickedness on the earth, and *he saw that everything they thought or imagined was consistently and totally evil.* Genesis 6:12 NLT

Spirits of Nephilim manifest in the same manner as depicted by the Nephilim nations. We still have these evil spirits instilling the same mindsets of corruption in modern times.

> ...That we might not have Satan get an advantage against us, for we are not ignorant of his thoughts. 2 Corinthians 2:11 Darby Bible Translation

A set way of thinking defines a mindset, and all cultures possess values and patterns of thoughts unique to it. Individuals develop mindsets by means of their families, religious beliefs, education, and all they observe through their lives. Mirror neurons imprint on our minds by what we see and hear.[109] If for example, sexual conduct with multiple sex partners imprints as normal in a society, then to that society it is normal. Whether it opposes God's Word or not, the next generation will most likely do the same.

> 2 But because of immoralities, each man is to have his own wife, and each woman is to have her own husband. 1 Corinthians 1:2 NASB

The Biblical account of Lot's daughters gives us a good example of those who lived around Nephilim practices and copied them. Lot's daughters got their father drunk, and both daughters conceived their sons by incest. Incest as we read was a practice of the Egyptians and Canaanites who were Nephilim seeded nations.

## Demonic Influence

> Because that, when they knew God, they glorified [him] not as God, neither were thankful; but became vain in their imaginations, and their foolish heart was darkened. Romans 1:21 KJV

Diabolical spirits transfer their mindsets to humans through fiery darts which come to humans as thoughts, impressions, or vain imaginations as well as through dreams and visions. Devils and demons seek to control generations with mindsets in opposition to God's word. Even though humans generate their own thoughts and desires, we tend not to recognize occurrences from the supernatural realm but believe all thoughts originate from within. I am not talking of someone whose brain chemistry does not function correctly or a mental illness, but of the effect of evil spirits, that may afflict these people as well.

> For from within, out of the heart of man, come evil thoughts, sexual immorality, theft, murder, adultery ... Mark 7:21 ESV

The world in which we live remains under the control of Satan who works by evil spirits through sinful mankind.

Matthew 8:28 described the account of demon possession in the region of Gerasenes with two men possessed with devils. *The Greek word for devil,* daimonizomai, *signifies "to be possessed of a demon, to act under the control of a demon. Those who were thus afflicted expressed the mind and consciousness of the "demon" or "demons" indwelling them."*[110] Consciousness denotes, "a sense of one's personal or collective identity, especially the complex of attitudes, beliefs, and sensitivities held by or considered characteristic of an individual or a group.[111] Evil spirits can access people to the point a demon or devil expresses its thoughts and consciousness through a person. People take on the personality traits of evil spirits believing and then confirming, "This is the way I am." When people agree and believe these lies, then the spirit may operate through them.

> We know that we are of God, and that the whole world lies in the power of the evil one. 1 John 5:19 NASB

Knowing God's Word and his guidelines for righteous living (Exodus 20) enables us to resist mindsets from Nephilim spirits. Stand guard against thoughts which oppose the truth of God's word and for one's individual life's plan given by God.

> Once you were dead because of your disobedience and your many sins. ² You used to live in sin, just like the rest of the world, obeying the devil—the commander of the powers in the unseen world. He is the spirit at work in the hearts of those who refuse to obey God. ³ All of us used to live that way, following the passionate desires and inclinations of our sinful nature. By our very nature we were

subject to God's anger, just like everyone else. Ephesians 2:1-3 NLT

Jesus speaking, "I know that you are Abraham's descendants; yet you seek to kill Me, because My word has no place in you. I speak the things which I have seen with My Father; therefore you also do the things which you *heard* from your father" (John 8:37-38 NASB).

"You are of *your* father the devil, and you want to do the desires of your father. He was a murderer from the beginning, and does not stand in the truth because there is no truth in him. Whenever he speaks a lie, he speaks from his own *nature,* for he is a liar and the father of lies. John 8:44 NASB

From Jesus' own words we understand humans do "hear" from the spirit realm because of this reference to the devil as their spiritual father.

A good person produces good things from the treasury of a good heart, and an evil person produces evil things from the treasury of an evil heart. What you say flows from what is in your heart. Luke 6:45 NLT

We must guard our thought life. Satanic attacks come to ensnare their victims. For example, a sudden desirous thought totally against your norm or of something you gave up years before could be a dart from the spirit realm. The New Testament calls such thoughts "fiery darts of the wicked one" (Ephesians 6:6b).

> Above all, taking the shield of faith, with which you shall be able to quench all the fiery darts of the wicked one. Ephesians 6:6 KJV

The enemy seeks to separate us from God's word. He also works to divide people one from another through a cloud of misunderstanding and miscommunication that prevails in the midst of a diabolical attack. Besieged, one may be falsely targeted or accused. In such an attack, anger flares as emotions get out of hand. All the while one wonders why this is happening. The way to stand against such a diabolical attack comes by ones faith in the Word of God and through obedience to the Holy Spirit's guidance. This may leave a victim astonished at what happened and even mad. Get away from the situation as soon as possible. If you find yourself in unforgiveness or in any other sin, repent and forgive, resist the devil, kick him out, and continue to resist the thoughts and vain imaginations. Speak the word of truth and allow the Holy Spirit to lead you into victory over such attacks.

> Submit yourselves, then, to God. Resist the devil, and he will flee from you. James 4:7 ESV

A demonic attack may also bring deception through confusion or a foggy mind that cannot think clearly. One who comes under an attack can become overwhelmed and bombarded with thoughts and imaginations they cannot seem to get rid of. An attempt to stop these thoughts finds an instant repeat of much the same. Make sure you walk in forgiveness, or sin does not remain concerning the topic of these thoughts. Out of the spirit realm whispers so subtle, a victim believes the thoughts and emotions originate from themselves.

> For as he thinks within himself, so is he. Proverbs 23:7 NASB

If deceptive thoughts prevail and finds acceptance by the victim, entrapment to the falsehood occurs and these thoughts become theirs.

> But he will pour out his anger and wrath on those who live for themselves, who refuse to obey the truth and instead live lives of wickedness. Romans 2: 8 NLT

When God and his Word are ignored, man's thoughts become futile. Futile thoughts are "of no importance; answering no useful end; useless; vain; worthless."[112]

> Guard your heart above all else, for it determines the course of your life. Proverbs 4:23 NLT

# Chapter 29

# Corruption of God's People

Throw off your old sinful nature and your former way of life, which is corrupted by lust and deception. Instead, let the Spirit renew your thoughts and attitudes. Ephesians 4:22NLT

Sons of God released a concentration of sins to lure mankind to lifestyles in opposition to the kingdom of God. In looking at God's commands of what not to do, we see what Nephilim nations did do.

## Unlawful Sexual Relations

1The LORD said to Moses, 2"Speak to the Israelites and say to them: 'I am the LORD your God. 3You must not do as they do in Egypt, where you used to live, and you must not do as they do in the land of Canaan, where I am bringing you. Do not follow their practices. *4You must obey my laws and be careful to follow my decrees.* I am the LORD your God. 5Keep my decrees and laws, for theman who obeys them will live by them. I am the LORD. 6"'No one is to approach any close relative to have sexual relations. I am the LORD. 20"'Do not have sexual relations with your neighbor's wife and defile yourself with her. 21"'Do not give any of your children to be sacrificed to Molech, for you must not profane the name of your God. I am the LORD. 22"'Do not lie with a man as one lies with a woman; that is detestable. 23"'Do not have sexual relations with an animal and defile yourself with it. A woman must not present herself to an animal to have sexual relations with it; that is a perversion. 24"'**Do not defile yourselves in any of these ways, because this is how the nations that I am going to drive out before you became defiled.** Leviticus 18:1-24

Notice both Egypt and Canaan participated in the same sexual practices because both were Nephilim seeded nations.

Spirits of the Nephilim push for sexual perversions to be normalized in order to teach the mindset of the Nephilim to the generations. Once the generations accept the perversion, their minds and thoughts are acceptable to devils and demons in opposition to God. This is one reason God kept telling Israel to stay away from sexual immorality and the pagan practices of the Nephilim nations, because of their open sexual sin. If ensnared, they would become just like the Canaanite nations, but they did not listen. Once they came in agreement and participated in the sins of the Nephilim nations, it became hard to tell the difference between God's children and the Nephilim.

> 35 But they mingled with the nations And learned their practices, 36 And served their idols, Which became a snare to them. 37 They even sacrificed their sons and their daughters to the demons, 38 And shed innocent blood, The blood of their sons and their daughters, Whom they sacrificed to the idols of Canaan; And the land was polluted with the blood. 39 Thus they became unclean in their practices, And played the harlot in their deeds. 40 Therefore the anger of the LORD was kindled against His people And He abhorred His inheritance. Psalm 106:35-40 NASB

Nephilim spirits promote religious practices to deceive and keep people from the truth; they achieve their goals by teaching doctrine of devils which goes back to what the sons of God taught daughters of men (1 Corinthians 10:21). Below are more "do nots" and ways of the Nephilim which God told his children not to duplicate. Notice the prevalence of some of these in our modern cultures which finds origins from the Nephilim.

> 4"'Do not turn to idols or make gods of cast metal for yourselves. I am the LORD your God. 19"'Keep my decrees. "'Do not mate different kinds of animals. "'Do not plant your field with two kinds of seed. "'Do not wear clothing woven of two kinds of material. 26"'Do not eat any meat with the blood still in it. "'Do not practice divination or sorcery. 27"'Do not cut the hair at the sides of your head or clip off the edges of your beard. 28"'Do not cut your bodies for the dead or put tattoo marks on yourselves. I am the LORD

29"'Do not degrade your daughter by making her a prostitute, or the land will turn to prostitution and be filled with wickedness. 31"'Do not turn to mediums or seek out spiritists, for you will be defiled by them.'" Leviticus 19:4-31

Sins of the Nephilim infested the generations before the flood and will continue until the second coming of Jesus Christ. Before the flood, we know only one preacher of righteousness was left on earth; they did a very thorough job.

### Open Immorality among God's People

1While Israel was staying in Shittim, the men began to indulge in sexual immorality with Moabite women, 2who invited them to the sacrifices to their gods. The people ate and bowed down before these gods. 3So Israel joined in worshiping the Baal of Peor. And the Lord anger burned against them.4The Lord said to Moses, "Take all the leaders of these people, kill them and expose them in broad daylight before the Lord, so that the Lord's fierce anger may turn away from Israel."5So Moses said to Israel's judges, "Each of you must put to death those of your men who have joined in worshiping the Baal of Peor." 6Then an Israelite man brought to his family a Midianite woman right before the eyes of Moses and the whole assembly of Israel while they were weeping at the entrance to the Tent of Meeting. 7When Phinehas son of Eleazar, the son of Aaron, the priest, saw this, he left the assembly, took a spear in his hand 8and followed the Israelite into the tent. He drove

> the spear through both of them—through the Israelite and into the woman's body. Then the plague against the Israelites was stopped; 9but those who died in the plague numbered 24,000. Numbers 25:1-9

A Holy God's anger fiercely burned against his people and 24,000 died as a result of the consequences of their sins (Romans 6:23). God's people did not discern the danger of their ways.

> When you enter the land the LORD your God is giving you, do not learn to imitate the detestable ways of the nations there. Deuteronomy 18:9

Nephilim people seduce in one form of the other, and God knew what would happen if his people got around them. "The men began to indulge in sexual immorality with Midianite women, who invited them to the sacrifices of their gods. The people ate and bowed down before these gods and joined their worship of Baal of Peor" (Numbers 25:1-3). Let's get some history from Keil and Delitzsch Biblical Commentary on how manipulation from the spirit realm worked through the Midianites.

> As the princes of Midian (who were allied to Moab) had been the advisers and assistants of the Moabitish king in the attempt to destroy the Israelites by a curse of God; so now, after the failure of that plan, they were the soul of the new undertaking *to weaken Israel and render it harmless, by seducing it to idolatry, and thus leading it into apostasy from its God.* But it was Balaam, as is afterwards casually observed in Numbers 31:16, who first of all gave this advice.

> This is passed over here, because the point of chief importance in relation to the object of the narrative was not Balaam's share in the proposal, but the carrying out of the proposal itself. The daughters of Moab, however, also took part in carrying it out, by forming friendly associations with the Israelites, and then inviting them to their sacrificial festival. They only are mentioned in Numbers 25:1, Numbers 25:2, as being the daughters of the land. The participation of the Midianites appears first of all in the shameless licentiousness of Cozbi, the daughter of the Midianitish prince, from which we not only see that the princes of Midian performed their part, but obtain an explanation of the reason why the judgment upon the crafty destroyers of Israel was to be executed upon the Midianites. [113]

This plainly demonstrates a standard plan of the Nephilim for our destruction: sexual and spiritual immorality which kindles God's righteous anger.

> Put to death, therefore, whatever belongs to your earthly nature: sexual immorality, impurity, lust, evil desires and greed, which is idolatry. Colossians 3:5

An Israelite man demonstrated he lacked fear of God when he brought a Midianite woman to the camp in full sight of Moses and the leaders of Israel. So let's review God's accomplishments through Moses, a prophet of God.

36 "This man led them out, performing wonders and signs in the land of Egypt and in the Red Sea and in the wilderness for forty years. 37 "This is the Moses who said to the sons of Israel, 'GOD WILL RAISE UP FOR YOU A PROPHET LIKE ME FROM YOUR BRETHREN.' 38 "This is the one who was in the congregation in the wilderness together with the angel who was speaking to him on Mount Sinai, and *who was* with our fathers; and he received living oracles to pass on to you. Acts 7:36-38 NASB

Immorality brought spiritual blindness and deception to the young man as he did not discern Moses, the man of God, or the time of judgment. Immorality had become accepted, and this man and woman had no shame.

Why did God command Moses to destroy the leaders? Leaders are held to a higher standard, and immorality seems to have gone on for a while to the point of affecting the entire community. Sexual immorality led to spiritual immorality that greatly aroused God's anger against Israel's leaders. The fear of God fell upon Moses and the judges because they knew God's judgment was at hand. Remember every time a child of God engages in immorality, they are mixing the Holy Spirit with the spirit of a harlot (devil), which is an atrocity. The Holy Spirit wars with these spirits, and God became enraged.

Moses and the leaders of the Israel knew God's standards of holiness could not bend for anyone. Jesus bore our sins and forgives those who repent of them but repent they must. Repent in Greek, metanoeo, means "repentance" from sin and a change of mind that involves both a turning from sin and a turning to God."[114]

# Chapter 30

# Nephilim Webb

There were even male and female shrine prostitutes throughout the land. The people imitated the detestable practices of the pagan nations the LORD had driven from the land ahead of the Israelites. 1 Kings 14:24 NLT

Prostitution (sexual immorality) became implanted on earth as a spiritual act of worship to pagan gods. Sexual immorality ties to spiritual immorality, which ties to oppression of God's people as we have seen. In modern times we see sexual immorality rampant and common place, even in the church.

Evil spirits seek to destroy the righteous by enticement to sin which also happened to King David (2 Samuel 11and12) who among all the kings of Israel had multiple wives. God commanded Israel not to marry women from the Nephilim nations because they would entice them to worship their false God's. Multiple wives did not originate from God. But by following his culture and the ways of kings instead of the decrees of God, King David's brought hardship on himself.

Look at King David's wives and his children by different women. A wife and her background directly influences a child and so a father. He conceived Solomon through Bathsheba, which reminds me; King David followed a Nephilim practice here as well: "see and take." He saw Bathsheba, and he took her, even though she was married. King David's attempt to hide their child's conception backfired when her husband would not sleep with his wife, so King David arranged his death. King David might have thought he'd gotten away with such sin, but it did not escape God who sent Nathan the prophet to King David. He repented only after being confronted.

King David was not a seed of the Nephilim but became seeded under the influence of Nephilim spirits due to the fact he opened the door to these spirits by his sin. What happened as a result? Judgment fell on King David and his family.

Generational problems also arose because of Nephilim spirits at work through his children. Among King David's wives were women of Nephilim nations. One of King David's sons, Annon, was a deceiver. In uncontained lust for his sister, he forced her into incest by rape and then kicked her out as trash. Another deceiver and son of King David, Absalom, also displayed behavior patterns and sins of Nephilim nations and diabolical Nephilum spirits.

King Solomon took wives from Egypt among other Nephilim nations. Because of his sexual connection to them, he became spiritually connected and worshipped false Gods (1 Kings 3:12).

1But king Solomon loved many strange women, together with the daughter of Pharaoh, women of the Moabites, Ammonites, Edomites, Zidonians, and Hittites; 2Of the nations *concerning* which the LORD said unto the children of Israel, Ye shall not go in to them, neither shall they come in unto you: *for* surely they will turn away your heart after their gods: Solomon clave unto these in love. 3And he had seven hundred wives, princesses, and three hundred concubines: and his wives turned away his heart. 4For it came to pass, when Solomon was old, *that* his wives turned away his heart after other gods: and his heart was not perfect with the LORD his God, as *was* the heart of David his father. 5For Solomon went after Ashtoreth the goddess of the Zidonians, and after Milcom the abomination of the Ammonites. 6And Solomon did evil in the sight of the LORD, and went not fully after the LORD, as *did* David his father. 7Then did Solomon build an high place for Chemosh, the abomination of Moab, in the hill that *is* before Jerusalem, and for Molech, the abomination of the children of Ammon. 8And likewise did he for all his strange wives, which burnt incense and sacrificed unto their gods. 9And the LORD was angry with Solomon, because his heart was turned from the LORD God of Israel, which had appeared unto him twice, 10And had commanded him concerning this thing, that he should not go after other gods: but he kept not that which the LORD commanded. 11Wherefore the LORD said unto Solomon, Forasmuch as this is done of thee, and thou hast not kept my covenant and my statutes, which I have commanded thee, I will surely rend the kingdom from thee, and will give it to thy servant. 12Notwithstanding in thy days I will not do it for David thy father's sake: *but* I will rend it out of the hand of thy son. 13Howbeit I will not rend away all the kingdom; *but* will give one tribe to thy son for David my servant's sake, and for Jerusalem's sake which I have chosen. 1 Kings 1:1-13 KJV

Who taught King Solomon such practices as these in 1 Kings 1:1-13? Nephilim women would not have given up on luring Solomon to their form of worship because ingrained in Nephilim will be seduction meant to destroy faith in the One True God. Through the sexual connection, idolatry flowed. What happened to King Solomon? He also came under judgment from God.

# Chapter 31

# Covenant

God gave mankind covenants, and we need to review their importance for our lives now and for eternity. A covenant can be easily understood as a contract between parties. Biblically, a covenant came about by a promise or promises given by God to an individual or a group of people, where certain behavior was required according to the conditions of their agreement. God made covenants with Adam, Noah, Abraham, and Moses, to name a few, along with the promise of salvation by faith in Jesus Christ. In all of these covenants, actions that came in line with the stipulations of the covenant received the benefit of the promise. In Adam's failure, he lost the benefit.[115]

"When men entered a covenant and God was called upon as a witness, it was known as a 'covenant of the Lord' (1 Sam. 20:8), and the marriage covenant made in God's name was known as 'the covenant of God'."[116] Any covenant of the kingdom of God succeeds when the guidelines of the kingdom are followed, but in human history this has not always been the case as Biblical accounts confirm.

11Judah has been unfaithful, and a detestable thing has been done in Israel and in Jerusalem. The men of Judah have defiled the LORD's beloved sanctuary by marrying women who worship idols. 12May the LORD cut off from the nation of Israel every last man who has done this and yet brings an offering to the LORD of Heaven's Armies. Malachi 2:11-12 NLT

13Here is another thing you do. You cover the LORD's altar with tears, weeping and groaning because he pays no attention to your offerings and doesn't accept them with pleasure. 14You cry out, "Why doesn't the LORD accept my worship?" I'll tell you why! Because the LORD witnessed the vows you and your wife made when you were young. But you have been unfaithful to her, though she remained your faithful partner, the wife of your marriage vows. 15Didn't the LORD make you one with your wife? In body and spirit you are his. And what does he want? Godly children from your union. So guard your heart; remain loyal to the wife of your youth. 16"For I hate divorce!" says the LORD, the God of Israel. "To divorce your wife is to overwhelm her with cruelty," says the LORD of Heaven's Armies. "So guard your heart; do not be unfaithful to your wife Malachi 2:13-16 NLT

Men of Judah (Jewish men) married women of a strange god. Just as they violated their spiritual covenant to God, some also became sexually unfaithful, broke their marriage covenants, and divorced their wives. Here in Malachi, this familiar pattern of spiritual and sexual immorality was at work once again. What did the Lord do with these men who did this? God cut them off from the people of God. These men were cut off but continued to bring offerings to the Lord. They did not know God cut them off. Why? These men were deceived by immorality as ones who could do what they wanted without consequence.

In a holy marriage covenant, a man and woman unite by a commitment to one another and to the Lord. God blesses as the couple submits to the stipulations of the covenant. If one breaks their covenantal vow, God's blessing lifts and his judgment comes.

> But if you do not obey the LORD, and if you rebel against his commands, his hand will be against you, as it was against your fathers. 1 Samuel 12:15

Based on morality, a marriage covenant forsakes all others, and, even though they are two people, they will be as one. Two shall become one is a sexual and a spiritual union. "Didn't the Lord make you one with your wife? In body and spirit you are his. And what does he want, Godly children from your union. So guard your heart; remain loyal to the wife of your youth" (Malachi 2:15).

By this spiritual covenant God extends his blessing over children, and they become holy. A believer should not have anything to do with fornication because it is outside the covenant of God, which is the place for unbelievers.

> Do not let any part of your body become an instrument of evil to serve sin. Instead, give yourselves completely to God, for you were dead, but now you have new life. So use your whole body as an instrument to do what is right for the glory of God. Romans 6:13

### Born Outside of Covenant

Children conceived outside of a marriage covenant are targets of Nephilim spirits. An example of covenantal protection goes back to Israel's exit from Egypt. The night before Moses lead the nation of Israel out of Egypt, they ate the Passover lamb. God instructed the Israelites to mark their houses with the blood of the lamb before judgment fell. Those who submitted to God's instruction covered their house with the blood and were kept safe. Those who did not have the blood were targets for destruction (Exodus 12:5-7:12-13).

> 13 *'The blood shall be a sign for you on the houses where you live*; and when I see the blood I will pass over you, and no plague will befall you to destroy *you* when I strike the land of Egypt. Exodus 12:13 NASB

As a part of the Abrahamic covenant in Genesis, chapter 15, Abraham's knew his seed would be in bondage for 400 years and then would be set free. God's timing is impeccable. On the exact day in the 400th year, God's people came out of bondage from Egypt (Genesis 15:13-14).

In a covenant with God, if one breaks a stipulation, repentance must occur before restoration can take place. Spiritual dullness covers those who engage in immorality. If one continues in this sin and ignores the Holy Spirit's pleadings to repent, a hard, unresponsive heart may arise. Within this process, Satan will seize opportunity to" kill, steal or destroy" through the door of unrepentant sin (John 10:10 NLT).

Satan does not like marriage in the form God created and seeks its transform or destruction. A marriage protects children by the watchful eyes of two parents. Children conceived outside of marriage may never enjoy a home with two parents and make it easier for Nephilim activities. A godly mother and father will guard their children and teach them Christian values, which Satan hates. Even in a single parent household, it takes a committed, watchful parent to protect a child. When parents are actively rearing their children in righteousness, trouble can be averted.

I bet the reader has heard this: "We are just trying out living together to see if it works for us," or "We just want to live together." Such statements come from the pit of hell and avails children to be born outside of covenant, game for Nephilim exploitation. Satan knew quite well what he was doing when he sent sexual perversion and immorality, as Satan's plan to destroy us all revolves around some type of immorality.

*1Hear this, O priests! Give heed, O house of Israel! Listen, O house of the king! For the judgment applies to you, For you have been a snare at Mizpah And a net spread out on Tbor. 2The revolters have gone deep in depravity, But I will chastise all of them. 3I know Ephraim, and Israel is not hidden from Me; For now, O Ephraim, you have played the harlot, Israel has defiled itself. 4Their deeds will not allow them to return to their God. For a spirit of harlotry is within them, And they do not know the LORD.* Hosea 5:1-7 NASB

God's leaders and his people fell by a spirit of harlotry, the same net of idolatry and sexual immorality as others before. The priest's job was to teach the law, and the king was to enforce the law. Both failed in their duties which brought deep depravity to people who no longer knew the Lord, and whose deeds kept them from him. God had enough, and his Presence withdrew from his people. Deceived and knew it not, they sought the Lord but could not find him. These people had polluted themselves because of immorality and became unclean. God's people could not return to him because they did not know he'd left. Those who thought they were God's people were no longer, as they stumbled in iniquity as their forefathers.

Hosea tells us God's people "dealt treacherously against the Lord, for they have borne illegitimate children" (Hosea 5:7). God's portions are his children, and, because of immorality, the children born were not God's. Two were to become one flesh in a covenant of marriage because God wanted holy children.

> ⁸ "For Abraham will certainly become a great and mighty nation, and all the nations of the earth will be blessed through him. ¹⁹ I have singled him out so that he will direct his sons and their families to keep the way of the LORD by doing what is right and just. Then I will do for Abraham all that I have promised." Genesis 18:18-19 NLT

As a part of the Abrahamic covenant, God's ways were to be taught to each generation to ensure they would know him and be known by God. In Hosea, God's people bore children out of immorality who were not taught the ways of God by their parents. Scripture calls them strange, as they were strangers to God (Hosea 5:7 KJ). Repetition of illegitimate children in the generations created those who did not know God, and he did not know them."[117]

## Violating Covenant

> His judgments are true and just. He has punished the great prostitute who corrupted the earth with her immorality. Revelations 19:2a NLT

Everything Satan set out to do through the rebellious sons of God he accomplished first by perverting sex. Sexual immorality is idolatry (Colossians 3:5). Nephilim worship through immoral sex acts, as immorality uses ones physical body as an instrument of worship.

In a simple way, it is like raising your hands in worship of God. We know Nephilim also use sexual immorality to seed more humans with spirits of Nephilim, and by the third and fourth generation extremely corrupt individuals emerge.

Spirits of Nephilim also seek human sacrifice. Abortion works as such, with many abortions occurring as a consequence of immorality.

Nephilim manifest differently through people according to the type of evil spirit which oppresses them. This factor is an accumulation of their sin and iniquity, along with environment, how and where they were reared, and mindsets and deception the enemy has sewn in them. Seed of the Nephilim find themselves different from other humans and mimic normal humans to go unnoticed. These are the ones that care nothing about any of us. They use us for their purposes, and if we suffer or die as a result, they do not care. Caring is not what they do. They are crossbreeds who lack a full human connection to the rest of us. Nephilim seed are on the rise in the earth and in all walks of life and professions. We need not be ignorant for they are alive and well on planet Earth.

Death, murder, mayhem, oppression, poverty, fear, and much human misery all goes back to one immoral angel, who sent immorality into our spirits, and then our physical bodies, through more immoral angels to oppress and rule mankind by Satan's kingdom.

# Chapter 32

## Preparation of the Bride

> Christ loved the church and gave himself up for her 26 to make her holy, cleansing her by the washing with water through the word, 27 and to present her to himself as a radiant church, without stain or wrinkle or any other blemish, but holy and blameless. Ephesians 5:25b-27

The Bride of Christ reflects him. She glories in his Presence. She radiates his holiness and illuminates his being, She loves him and he loves her; he is her Lord, she is his body. She is as he, for his word fills her in every way. The Bride of Christ embodies the Word of God for the two became one, just as a man and his wife.

In the Bride of Christ there is holiness- no immorality, no idolatry, no rebellion. Who wants to marry a prostitute? Who wants to join themselves to the unfaithful, one who sleeps with anyone and brings filth back to them? Who wants to marry one who lies and continues to rebel? Would Christ join himself to a sorcerer, a murder, a liar, a deceiver, or an idol worshiper? No, he would not; he could not, for these are of another kingdom.

> "Why do you call Me, 'Lord, Lord,' and do not do what I say? Luke 6:46 NASB

Recall Satan mimics God's kingdom. As the Lord calls out to his children to make themselves ready, Satan moves upon his seed to infiltrate and weaken those who call upon the name of the Lord. As the Lord prepares to join his bride, Satan prepares his bride as well. Our problem, the bride of Satan has intermingled with the church, the work of the Nephilim.

# Chapter 33

## Bride of Deceit – Fakes in our Midst

> Watch out for those dogs, those people who do evil, those mutilators who say you must be circumcised to be saved.
> Philippians 3:2 NLT

Out of Satan's kingdom comes his bride. She bears his resemblance the closest. By the works of the Nephilim, Satan receives children in his image; his bride comes out of them. Satan's bride reflects him, the sexually immoral, idolaters, adulterers, male or female prostitutes, sexual offenders, cowards, unbelievers, the corrupt, murderers, those who practice witchcraft, and all liars (Rev 21:8; 1 Corinthians 6:9). Satan is the father of deceit, a liar from the beginning. Everything the Lord is, he is not. He masquerades as an angel of light as does his bride. Jesus explains among us are those who look like us but are not.

## Parable of Tares

24Jesus told them another parable: "The kingdom of heaven is like a man who sowed good seed in his field. 25But while everyone was sleeping, his enemy came and sowed weeds among the wheat, and went away. 26When the wheat sprouted and formed heads, then the weeds also appeared. 27"The owner's servants came to him and said, 'Sir, didn't you sow good seed in your field? Where then did the weeds come from?' 28"'An enemy did this,' he replied. "The servants asked him, 'Do you want us to go and pull them up?' 29"'No,' he answered, 'because while you are pulling the weeds, you may root up the wheat with them. 30Let both grow together until the harvest. At that time I will tell the harvesters: First collect the weeds and tie them in bundles to be burned; then gather the wheat and bring it into my barn.'" Matthew 13:24-30 NASB

"The field is the world; the good seed are the children of the kingdom; but the tares are the sons of the evil one, the seed of Satan" Matthew 13:38 KJV.

36Then He left the crowds and went into the house. And His disciples came to Him and said, "Explain to us the parable of the tares of the field." 37And He said, "The one who sows the good seed is the Son of

Man, 38and the field is the world; and as for the good seed, these are the sons of the kingdom; and *the tares are the sons of the evil one; 39and the enemy who sowed them is the devil,* and the harvest is the end of the age; and the reapers are angels. 40"So just as the tares are gathered up and burned with fire, so shall it be at the end of the age. 41"*The Son of Man will send forth His angels, and they will gather out of His kingdom all stumbling blocks, and those who commit lawlessness, 42and will throw them into the furnace of fire; in that place there will be weeping and gnashing of teeth.* 43"Then THE RIGHTEOUS WILL SHINE FORTH AS THE SUN in the kingdom of their Father. He who has ears, let him hear. Matthew 13:36-43 NASB

The Jewish New Testament Commentary connects tares to prostitution in the time before the flood when the entire earth corrupted their way. Tares are "zonah" ("prostitutes') or the immoral that produce and reproduce the Nephilim seed throughout the generations.[118]

Seed of the Nephilim and those seeded by them behave the same as those described in Genesis chapter 6. Nephilim mindsets and accompanying behavior have become so blended into society and picked up with complacency in the church. As the blood bought church, we are made in the image and likeness of Christ. He is our life, and when he appears we will be like him. How can we be like him if some act like the Nephilim?

> 9Don't you realize that those who do wrong will not inherit the Kingdom of God? Don't fool yourselves. Those who indulge in sexual sin, or who worship idols, or commit adultery, or are male prostitutes, or practice homosexuality, 10 or are thieves, or greedy people, or drunkards, or are abusive, or cheat people—none of these will inherit the Kingdom of God. 11Some of you were once like that. But you were cleansed; you were made holy; you were made right with God by calling on the name of the Lord Jesus Christ and by the Spirit of our God. 1 Corinthians 6:9-11 NLT

The Bride of Christ submits to the Word of God and becomes radiantly clean, without any blemish. The false bride does not submit to God's Word, only as a pretense, but truly not at all. The New Testament church became inundated by these pretenders, so we need to be able to tell the difference between the good and the bad seed. Recall again, some Nephilim are religious and drawn to it. They love to think of themselves as the enlightened ones in any situation, but their actions are the same as they always have been. They are so engrained in deception; they deceive even themselves and believe they are righteous but according to their own worldly standards.

> 17 Now I urge you, brethren, keep your eye on those who cause dissensions and hindrances contrary to the teaching which you learned, and turn away from them.

> 18 For such men are slaves, not of our Lord Christ but of their own appetites; and by their smooth and flattering speech they deceive the hearts of the unsuspecting. Romans 16:17-18 NASB

Christians described as sheep are inclined to be unsuspecting of pretenders. We take people at their word and tend not to inspect others' lives. The seed of the Nephilim take advantage of our weakness.

> ⁶For among them are those who worm their way into homes and captivate silly and weak natured and spiritually dwarfed women, loaded down with [the burden of their] sins [and easily] swayed and led away by various evil desires and seductive impulses. 2 Timothy 3:6 Amplified Bible (AMP)

In 2 Timothy 3:6, we see how pretenders take advantage of weak women, but take out the word "women" and look at what kind of target unsuspecting people become.

> They are the kind who work their way into people's lives* and win the confidence of vulnerable people* ... Timothy 3:6a NLT (*my adjustment)

We do not like to think that some people may be in our lives just to work some scheme, "by smooth and flattering speech, they deceive the unsuspecting," but this is how they operate (Romans 16:18 NASB).

## By Their Fruit Recognition Comes

> ¹⁵"Beware of false prophets who come disguised as harmless sheep but are really vicious wolves. ¹⁶ You can identify them by their fruit, that is, by the way they act. Can you pick grapes from thorn bushes, or figs from thistles? ¹⁷ A good tree produces good fruit, and a bad tree produces bad fruit. ¹⁸ A good tree can't produce bad fruit, and a bad tree can't produce good fruit. ¹⁹ So every tree that does not produce good fruit is chopped down and thrown into the fire. ²⁰ Yes, just as you can identify a tree by its fruit, so you can identify people by their actions. Matthew 7:15-20 NLT

They look like sheep but are wolves in sheep clothing. By the way they act, one can identify them, but this presents the problem; how they act in public view is much different than when out of sight. Seed of the Nephillim do not want to be detected and work their destruction behind the scenes. The facade they portray when others see will be what is expected, but out of sight they will satisfy their lustful natures and seduce others into their traps.

> 1There will be terrible times in the last days. 2People will be lovers of themselves, lovers of money, boastful, proud, abusive, disobedient to their parents, ungrateful, unholy, 3without love, unforgiving, slanderous, without self- control, brutal, not lovers of the good, 4treacherous, rash, conceited, lovers of pleasure rather

than lovers of God— 5having a form of godliness but denying its power. Have nothing to do with them. 2 Timothy 3:1-5 NIV

In the last days Nephilim philosophy, corruption, and violence permeate earth as it did prior to the flood. It was because of their presence the whole earth came under judgment. "When the Son of Man returns, it will be like it was in Noah's day" (Luke 17:26 NLT).

Paul gave Timothy the best advice on how to live around the Nephilim. "Have nothing to do with them" (2 Timothy 3:5). Once it is determined that someone is a seed of the Nephilim, get away from them or the situation as soon as possible.

The church is especially targeted by their antics. Look at what Jesus said about the Pharisees. They looked perfectly normal by their appearance, but on the inside they were full of "hypocrisy and lawlessness" (Matthew 23:28).

> 27"Woe to you, scribes and Pharisees, hypocrites! For you are like whitewashed tombs which on the outside appear beautiful, but inside they are full of dead men's bones and all uncleanness. 28 So you, too, outwardly appear righteous to men, but inwardly you are full of hypocrisy and lawlessness. Matthew 23:27-28 NASB

And the Lord was not done; read a little more of what he said.

> Then Jesus spoke to the crowds and to His disciples, ² saying: "The scribes and the Pharisees have seated themselves in the chair of Moses; ³ therefore all that they tell you, do and observe, but do not do according to their deeds; for they say *things* and do not do *them*. Matthew 23:1-3 NASB

These folks talk it, but do not walk it, and Jesus calls them "hypocrites and sons of hell" (Matthew 23:13-15).

### Accusers of the Brethren

Let me interject another facet of the Nephilim that needs to be understood: they are hypocrites who accuse others of what they themselves are guilty of doing. When they accuse another, they do not care if it's true or not. Harm to others is Nephilim residue. Victims will be lured into a trap and enticed to do wrong. Once done, they will expose the victim as the wrongdoer. Accusations are to get focus off them and destroy another. Jesus was accused of evil and sent to the cross. The accusations were false and meant to cause his death. The promise he would rise again had already been spoken (Matthew 27:63). Nothing stopped the Word of the Lord.

# Son of Hell

"Woe to you, teachers of the law and Pharisees, you hypocrites! You travel over land and sea to win a single convert, and when he becomes one, you make him twice as much a son of hell as you are." Matthew 23: 15

Jesus called these leaders "sons of hell" and exposed them. Nephilim release confusion by their hypocrisy and their spiritual entourage. Not only are these impostors in our congregations, they are among our leaders and about us in our everyday lives. Those who live by faith in submission to the Word of God and are led by the Spirit of God will overcome them. Build your life on the Rock, and these destructive forces cannot prevail against you (Matthew 7:26-27).

Paul, Peter, and Jude knew these people, their origins, and how much harm they cause. Today's church must not be ignorant of their devices.

> [4]For certain individuals whose condemnation was written about long ago have secretly slipped in among you. **They are *ungodly people, who pervert the grace of our God into a license for immorality* and deny Jesus Christ our only Sovereign and Lord.**[5] Though you already know all this, I want to remind you that the Lord at one time delivered his people out of Egypt, but later destroyed those who did not believe. Jude 1:4-5

11Woe to them! For they have gone the way of Cain, and for pay they have rushed headlong into the error of Balaam, and perished in the rebellion of Korah. 12These are the men who are hidden reefs in your love feasts when they feast with you without fear, caring for themselves; clouds without water, carried along by winds; autumn trees without fruit, doubly dead, uprooted; 13wild waves of the sea, casting up their own shame like foam; wandering stars, for whom the black darkness has been reserved forever. Jude 1:11-13, 16 NASB

# Chapter 34

## Enemy of Righteousness

The seed and those seeded of the Nephilim interfere with the kingdom of God at any opportunity.

> 6Afterward they traveled from town to town across the entire island until finally they reached Paphos, where they met a Jewish sorcerer, a false prophet named Bar-Jesus. 7He had attached himself to the governor, Sergius Paulus, who was an intelligent man. The governor invited Barnabas and Saul to visit him, for he wanted to hear the word of God. 8But Elymas, the sorcerer (as his name means in Greek), interfered and urged the governor to pay no attention to what Barnabas and Saul said. He was trying to keep the governor from believing. 9Saul, also known as Paul, was filled with the Holy Spirit, and he looked the sorcerer in the eye. 10Then he said, "You son of the devil, full of every sort of deceit and fraud, and enemy of all that is good! Will you never stop perverting the true ways of the Lord? Acts 13:6-10 NLT

Elymas, a sorcerer, actively sought to hinder a man's faith in salvation through Jesus Christ. Nephilim work to divide people from the truth and manipulate by sorcery to get the job done. False prophets will in one way or another pervert the true ways of God."

> 1 But the Spirit explicitly says that in later times some will fall away from the faith, paying attention to deceitful spirits and doctrines of demons, 2 by means of the hypocrisy of liars seared in their own conscience as with a branding iron 1Timoithy 4:1-2a NASB

Paul exposes this Nephilim seed, "*You son of the devil*, full of every *sort of deceit and fraud, and enemy of all that is good!* Will you never stop perverting the true ways of the Lord?" (Acts 13:10 NLT). Jannes, Jambres, and Elymas were sorcerers and men of corrupt minds, who stood in the way of God's purposes. Paul adds, and so do I, "As far as the faith is concerned, the seed of the Nephilim are rejected."

> Just as Jannes and Jambres opposed Moses, so these men also oppose the truth, men of depraved mind, rejected in regard to the faith. 2 Timothy 3:8 NASB

Actions of Nephilim seed or those under their influence are well described in 2 Peter 2.

> 1 But false prophets also arose among the people, just as there will also be false teachers among you, who will secretly introduce destructive heresies, even

denying the Master who bought them ... 2 Many will follow their sensuality, and because of them the way of the truth will be maligned; 3 and in their greed they will exploit you with false words...10 (they)* indulge the flesh in *its* corrupt desires and despise authority. 13They count it a pleasure to revel in the daytime. They are stains and blemishes, reveling in their deceptions, as they carouse with you, 14having eyes full of adultery that never cease from sin, enticing unstable souls, having a heart trained in greed, accursed children; 15forsaking the right way, 17 These are springs without water and mists driven by a storm, for whom the black darkness has been reserved. 18 For speaking out arrogant *words* of vanity they entice by fleshly desires, by sensuality, those who barely escape from the ones who live in error, 19 promising them freedom while they themselves are slaves of corruption; for by what a man is overcome, by this he is enslaved. 2 Peter 2:1a, 2, 3a, 13b-15a, 17-19 NASB

Mindsets that oppose the truth of God's word will lead a person toward acceptance of what the Nephilim instill in society. Nephilim seed are dead on the inside, just as Jesus said of the Pharisees. We must realize that not all called the church truly are the Church.

# Chapter 35

# Sifting

> 31 "Simon, Simon, behold, Satan has demanded *permission* to sift you like wheat; 32 but I have prayed for you, that your faith may not fail; and you, when once you have turned again, strengthen your brothers." Luke 22:31-32 NASB

God allows Satan to sift men in order to determine what is in a person. Ultimately it reveals those who are righteous and who are not. A new heaven and earth will be the home of the righteous only, so a sifting process continues to find genuine faith in the gift of eternal life through Jesus Christ.

## Good Fruit

In the Parable of the Sower, Jesus explains what happens when different people hear the word of the Kingdom of God (Matthew 13:3-9).

18 "Hear then the parable of the sower. 19 "When anyone hears the word of the kingdom and does not understand it, the evil *one* comes and snatches away what has been sown in his heart. This is the one on whom seed was sown beside the road. 20 "The one on whom seed was sown on the rocky places, this is the man who hears the word and immediately receives it with joy; 21 yet he has no *firm* root in himself, but is *only* temporary, and when affliction or persecution arises because of the word, immediately he falls away. 22 "And the one on whom seed was sown among the thorns, this is the man who hears the word, and the worry of the world and the deceitfulness of wealth choke the word, and it becomes unfruitful. 23 "And the one on whom seed was sown on the good soil, this is the man who hears the word and understands it; who indeed bears fruit and brings forth, some a hundredfold, some sixty, and some thirty." Matthew 13:18-23 NASB

A seed of faith is just that. It is not yet a plant or fruit but just a seed. If the seed gets proper soil, water, and nutrients, it will grow into what it is designed to be. When the Word of the Kingdom of God is sewn in a person's heart, a battle ensues as evil forces seek to destroy the seed of faith. In this parable there are four responses to the seed of faith. The first understands nothing and keeps nothing; the second receives with joy, but the seed is temporary and falls away at persecution and conflict because of the word. The third response hears the word, but these people are in tune with worldly worries along with deceit that comes with wealth, and the seed of faith does not bear any fruit. With no fruit or deeds of righteousness, no proof exists of genuine faith.

> 6Then Jesus told this story: "A man planted a fig tree in his garden and came again and again to see if there was any fruit on it, but he was always disappointed. 7Finally, he said to his gardener, 'I've waited three years, and there hasn't been a single fig! Cut it down. It's just taking up space in the garden.' 8"The gardener answered, 'Sir, give it one more chance. Leave it another year, and I'll give it special attention and plenty of fertilizer. 9If we get figs next year, fine. If not, then you can cut it down.'" Luke 13:6-9 NLT

We can tell an apple tree by the apples it produces, just as with fruit from any other tree. So when people claim they are believers, and do not bear any fruit of righteousness, are they really believers? Every person who does not produce good fruit will end up in the fire.

> Even now the ax of God's judgment is poised, ready to sever the roots of the trees. Yes, every tree that does not produce good fruit will be chopped down and thrown into the fire." Luke 3:9 NLT

The fourth response to the seed finds good soil where the message of the kingdom is heard, understood, and bears good fruit in the life of the true believer. Believers bear different amounts of fruit, but there is good fruit production (Galatians 5:22-23). These are the ones that no one can snatch from the hand of God (John 10:27-30).

> He cuts off every branch of mine that doesn't produce fruit, and he prunes the branches that do bear fruit so they will produce even more. John 15:2 NLT

Notice branches that produce good fruit will be pruned to produce more, but branches without any fruit will be cut off from the tree. Just as a branch that separates from a tree dies, so it is with anyone who does not remain in the Lord. Righteous fruit cannot come without abiding in Jesus. Fruitlessness is a telltale sign of the condition of the heart. Bad fruit designates a bad tree which also warrants cutting down and fire (Galatians 5:19-20).

> 4 "Abide in Me, and I in you. As the branch cannot bear fruit of itself unless it abides in the vine, so neither *can* you unless you abide in Me. John 15:4 NASB

> 5 "I am the vine, you are the branches; he who abides in Me and I in him, he bears much fruit, for apart from Me you can do nothing. John 5:3 NASB

6 "If anyone does not abide in Me, he is thrown away as a branch and dries up; and they gather them, and cast them into the fire and they are burned. John 15: 6 NASB

Nephilim are Satan's soldiers. They are seducers, deceivers, impostors, false ministers, teachers of heresy, and hypocrites who set traps to deceive the elect. Nephilim seed may seemingly produce fruit, but it's the plastic kind that sits in a dish to look good but nourishes no one.

# Chapter 36

## Faith Upholds the Commandments

We cannot gain salvation by the law, but by our faith in Jesus Christ we "uphold the law" Romans 3:31.

Even when we were dead in sins, hath quickened us together with Christ, (by grace ye are saved ;) Ephesians 2:5 KJ

21But now apart from the law the righteousness of God has been made known, to which the Law and the Prophets testify. 22 This righteousness is given through faith in Jesus Christ to all who believe. God presented Christ as a sacrifice of atonement through the shedding of his blood —to be received by faith.28 For we maintain that a person is justified by faith apart from the works of the law. 31 Do we, then, nullify the law by this faith? Not at all! Rather, we uphold the law. Romans 3:21, 22, 25, 28, 31

## The Ten Commandments

1And God spoke all these words: 2"I am the LORD your God, who brought you out of Egypt, out of the land of slavery. 3"You shall have no other gods before me. 4"You shall not make for yourself an idol in the form of anything in heaven above or on the earth beneath or in the waters below. 5You shall not bow down to them or worship them; 7"You shall not misuse the name of the LORD your God, for the LORD will not hold anyone guiltless who misuses his name. 8"Remember the Sabbath day by keeping it holy. 12"Honor your father and your mother, so that you may live long in the land the LORD your God is giving you. 13"You shall not murder. 14"You shall not commit adultery. 15"You shall not steal. 16"You shall not give false testimony against your neighbor. 17"You shall not covet your neighbor's house. You shall not covet your neighbor's wife, or his manservant or maidservant, his ox or donkey, or anything that belongs to your neighbor." Exodus 20:1-5, 7-8, 12-17

God gave Moses these Ten Commandments for the covenant with his people. Jesus Christ fulfilled all the requirements of the law which sinful man could not (2 Corinthians 5:21). By theses commandments, with the fruit of the Spirit in mind (Galatians 5:22-23), one may determine fruit production in a person's life. The life of a righteous person will conform to these written on their heart (John 15:1-27).

¹⁰ This is the covenant I will establish with the people of Israel after that time, declares the Lord. *I will put my laws in their minds and write them on their hearts.* I will be their God, and they will be my people. Hebrews 8:10

People quite frequently say one thing and do another. What a person believes is demonstrated by what they do. Faith in Jesus Christ will be seen by how a person lives their life.

3By this we know that we have come to know Him, if we keep His commandments. 4The one who says, "I have come to know Him," and does not keep His commandments, is a liar, and the truth is not in him; 5but whoever keeps His word, in him the love of God has truly been perfected. By this we know that we are in Him: 6the one who says he abides in Him ought himself to walk in the same manner as He walked. 1 John 2:3-6 NASB

Proof

21 Therefore, putting aside all filthiness and all that remains of wickedness, in humility receive the word implanted, which is able to save your souls. **22 But prove yourselves doers of the word, and not merely hearers who delude themselves.** 23 For if anyone is a hearer of the word and not a doer, he is like a man who looks at his natural face in a mirror;

> 24 for once he has looked at himself and gone away, he has immediately forgotten what kind of person he was. **25 But one who looks intently at the perfect law, the law of liberty, and abides by it, not having become a forgetful hearer but an effectual doer, this man will be blessed in what he does.** James 1:22-25 NASB

True believers bear the image of Christ by their faith and their deeds.

> 14 What good is it, my brothers and sisters, if someone claims to have faith but has no deeds? Can such faith save them? James 2:14

As we see in 2 Peter 2:21, people who turn away from the commandments become entangled in the world once again.

> 20 For if, after they have escaped the defilements of the world by the knowledge of the Lord and Savior Jesus Christ, they are again entangled in them and are overcome, the last state has become worse for them than the first. **21 For it would be better for them not to have known the way of righteousness, than having known it, to turn away from the holy commandment handed on to them.** 22 It has happened to them according to the true proverb, "A DOG RETURNS TO ITS OWN VOMIT," and, "A sow, after washing, *returns* to wallowing in the mire." 2 Peter 2:20-22 NASB

26Dear friends, if we deliberately continue sinning after we have received knowledge of the truth, there is no longer any sacrifice that will cover these sins. 27There is only the terrible expectation of God's judgment and the raging fire that will consume his enemies. Hebrews 10:24-25 NLT

# Chapter 37

# Sealing

God the Father placed his seal of approval on Jesus Christ (John 6:27).

A seal is "a private marking for security, protection, which maybe literally or figuratively and provides proof of authenticity."[119] [120] A seal also indicates ownership.[121]

> [27]Do not work for the food which perishes, but for the food which endures to eternal life, which the Son of Man will give to you, for on Him the Father, God, has set His seal." John 6:27 NASB

Those who accept Jesus Christ as Lord and Savior are sealed by the Holy Spirit as a deposit that guarantees their full redemption that will come.

> [13] In Him you also who have heard the Word of Truth, the glad tidings (Gospel) of your salvation, and have believed in *and* adhered to *and* relied on Him, were stamped with the seal of the long-promised Holy Spirit. [14] That [Spirit] is the guarantee of our inheritance [the

> first fruits, the pledge and foretaste, the down payment on our heritage], in anticipation of its full redemption *and* our acquiring [complete] possession of it—to the praise of His glory. Ephesians 1:13-14 Amplified Bible

> 21It is God who enables us, along with you, to stand firm for Christ. He has commissioned us, 22and he has identified us as his own by placing the Holy Spirit in our hearts as the first installment that guarantees everything he has promised us. 2 Corinthians 1:21b-22 NLT

> Now it is God who has made us for this very purpose and has given us the Spirit as a deposit, guaranteeing what is to come. 2 Corinthians 5:5

Before the end of this age, servants of the living God will be sealed by the work of angels (Revelations 7:2). True believers are already sealed by the Holy Spirit; even so, a seal of the living God is placed in the foreheads of God's servants before the four angels of Revelations chapter seven are allowed to harm the earth and sea.

> 1And after these things I saw four angels standing on the four corners of the earth, holding the four winds of the earth, that the wind should not blow on the earth, nor on the sea, nor on any tree. 2And I saw another angel ascending from the east, having the seal of the living God: and he cried with a loud voice to the four angels, to whom it was given to hurt the

earth and the sea, 3Saying, Hurt not the earth, neither the sea, nor the trees, till we have sealed the servants of our God in their foreheads. Revelation 7:1-3 KJV

Further along in Revelations chapter 9, we read of those who did not have the seal of the living God and became targets of tormenting spirits coming up out of the abyss.

> 3Then locusts came from the smoke and descended on the earth, and they were given power to sting like scorpions. 4They were told not to harm the grass or plants or trees, but only the people who did not have the seal of God on their foreheads. Revelations 9:3-4 NLT

No one can snatch a true, sealed believer from God's hand.

> 27"My sheep hear My voice, and I know them, and they follow Me; 28and I give eternal life to them, and they will never perish; and no one will snatch them out of My hand. 29"My Father, who has given *them* to Me, is greater than all; and no one is able to snatch *them* out of the Father's hand. 30"I and the Father are one." John 10:27-30 NASB

# Chapter 38

## Signs of the End of this Age

> Dear children, the last hour is here. You have heard that the Antichrist is coming, and already many such antichrists have appeared. From this we know that the last hour has come. 1 John 2:18 NLT

The Falling Away of the Church and the Antichrist

At a set time the Lord Jesus Christ will return to gather his elect to be with him.

> "As Jesus was sitting on the Mount of Olives, the disciples came to him privately. 'Tell us,' they said, 'when will this happen, and what will be the sign of your coming and of the end of the age?' Jesus answered: 'Watch out that no one deceives you. For many will come in my name, claiming, 'I am the Christ, and will deceive many. You will hear of wars and rumors of wars, but see to it that you are not alarmed. Such things must happen, but the end is still to come. Nation will rise against nation, and kingdom against

kingdom. There will be famines and earthquakes in various places. All these are the beginning of birth pains'" (Matthew 24:3-8). "Let no man deceive you by any means: for that day shall not come, except there come the falling away first, and that man of sin be revealed, the son of perdition" (2 Thessalonians 2:3 KJ).

We read that no one can snatch a true believer from the palm of the Lord's hand, so what is this falling away? This verse in the Ampflied Bible says this apostasy is the "falling away of those who have professed to be Christians" (2Thessalonians 2:3 KJ). Professed is the word that gives us a clue. Anybody can say he or she is a Christian, but as this book points out, there must be more than that. By its definition, "to lay claim to, often insincerely and pretend to," profession can be genuine or a pretense. [122]People can say anything about themselves, but there must be evidence. If someone needs a surgeon there should be proof of education and skills. It would be foolish to trust words alone because impostors have posed as heart surgeons, plastic surgeons, neurosurgeon as well as others. Those who pose as something they're not are deceivers.

False workers of Satan's kingdom will wow those on earth by "great signs and miracles to deceive even the elect-- if that were possible" (Matthew 24:24). We know false workers are either Nephilim seed or seeded individuals. As Satan's earthly soldiers, they work under the power of their spirit realm counterparts, devils, and demons. The elect are held and protected by God and will not budge from their faith in Jesus Christ. Nevertheless, believers will be under spiritual pressure from Satanic influences to do so (Matthew 24:24) "Deceivers are those who do not acknowledge Jesus Christ as coming in the flesh and have gone out into the world. Any such person is the deceiver and the antichrist" (2 John 1:7).

Apostasy defined is "an abandonment of what one has professed; a total desertion, or departure from one's faith or religion." [123] To this definition add the meaning of its Greek root word, *apostasion;* "divorce or repudiation, which is to cast off; to disavow; to have nothing to do with; to renounce; to reject." [124]

By putting these words together, we may recognize decisive actions of those who fall away. With such strong descriptive words, no wonder this "falling away" has been translated as the revolt or great rebellion against God.[125] Divorce cuts off family ties, and those who apostatize find it no longer beneficial to call themselves Christians. The falling away takes these "professed Christians" and severs their connections with the elect. "They went out from us, but they did not really belong to us. "For if they had belonged to us, they would have remained with us; but their going showed that none of them belonged to us" (1 John 2:19).

"The Son of Man will send forth His angels, and they will gather out of His kingdom all stumbling blocks and those who commit lawlessness" (Matthew 13:41KJ). The Ampflied Bible identifies stumbling blocks as "persons by whom others are drawn into error or sin." "And those who commit lawlessness for those who do iniquity and act wickedly" (Matthew 13:41). Satan sewed these rebellious ones among God's people and before the Lord comes back, they must be removed.

Faith in the name of Jesus stirs up hatred, brings imprisonment, and even death (Mark 13:11-13). "You will be handed over to be persecuted and put to death, and you will be hated by all nations because of me. At that time many will turn away from the faith and will betray and hate each other, and many false prophets will appear and deceive many people. Because of the increase of wickedness, the love of most will grow cold, but he who stands firm to the end will be saved. And this gospel of the kingdom will be preached in the whole world as a testimony to all nations, and then the end will come" (Matthew 24:9-14).

As persecution arises, pretenders and the non-committed run away. They do not love the truth to be saved, so God provides them with a delusion that seals their fate (2 Thessalonians 2:10). Upon rejection of the truth, they accept the influence of a delusion which the spirit of antichrist provides. Those with genuine faith stand firm in their love for their Lord and Savior Jesus Christ.

> "About the coming of our Lord Jesus Christ and how we will be gathered to meet him. For that day will not come until there is a great rebellion against God and the man of lawlessness is revealed—the one who brings destruction. He will exalt himself and defy everything that people call god and every object of worship. He will even sit in the temple of God, claiming that he himself is God. Don't you remember that I told you about all this when I was with you? And you know what is holding him back, for he can be revealed only when his time comes. For this lawlessness is already at work secretly,

and it will remain secret until the one who is holding it back steps out of the way. Then the man of lawlessness will be revealed, but the Lord Jesus will kill him with the breath of his mouth and destroy him by the splendor of his coming. This man will come to do the work of Satan with counterfeit power and signs and miracles. He will use every kind of evil deception to fool those on their way to destruction, because they refuse to love and accept the truth that would save them. So God will cause them to be greatly deceived, and they will believe these lies. They will be condemned for enjoying evil rather than believing the truth" (2 Thessalonians 2:1-11 NLT).

May the reader pay attention once again? End time events take place on God's time table, and the antichrist will appear at a set time (2 Thessalonians 2:6). The antichrist shows up first declaring he is the Messiah. Then Jesus, the true Redeemer, comes to slay him with "the breath of his mouth and destroys him by the splendor of his coming" (2 Thessalonians 2:8) So the man who sits in the temple and exalts himself as god above all that is called god is a fake. Satan has sought this moment from the time iniquity was conceived in his heart.

# Chapter 39

# The Bride Must Be Ready!

The Bride of Christ must make herself ready for the coming of our Lord. It is the hour to repent while you still have time. In Noah's day, once the rain began those outside the ark could not be saved, the time was up. No man knows the day or the hour of the return of the Lord, so each believer must be ready.

### That Day and Hour

> 36"But of that day and hour no one knows, not even the angels of heaven, nor the Son, but the Father alone. 37"For the coming of the Son of Man will be just like the days of Noah. 38"For as in those days before the flood they were eating and drinking, marrying and giving in marriage, until the day that Noah entered the ark, 39and they did not understand until the flood came and took them all away; so will the coming of the Son of Man be. Matthew 24:32-39 NASB

## Be on the Alert

42 "Therefore be on the alert, for you do not know which day your Lord is coming. 43 "But be sure of this, that if the head of the house had known at what time of the night the thief was coming, he would have been on the alert and would not have allowed his house to be broken into. 44 "For this reason *you also must be ready*; for the Son of Man is coming at an hour when you do not think *He will.* Matthew 24:42-44 NASB

## Be Faithful to the End

45"Who then is the faithful and wise servant, whom the master has put in charge of the servants in his household to give them their food at the proper time? 46It will be good for that servant whose master finds him doing so when he returns. 47I tell you the truth, he will put him in charge of all his possessions. 48But suppose that servant is wicked and says to himself, 'My master is staying away a long time,' 49and he then begins to beat his fellow servants and to eat and drink with drunkards. 50The master of that servant will come on a day when he does not expect him and at an hour he is not aware of. 51He will cut him to pieces and assign him a place with the hypocrites, where there will be weeping and gnashing of teeth. Matthew 24:45-51

When the master unexpectedly returned, each servant received accordingly. The first servant was found faithful even with his master's surprise arrival, and he would be rewarded. The second man, also a servant, could have been rewarded yet his deeds turned evil. This servant possibly thought he could live like he wanted and change before his master returned or his master would not know. Nonetheless, unannounced his master returned and assigned him with the hypocrites in eternal punishment.

> 28 Do not marvel at this; for an hour is coming, in which all who are in the tombs will hear His voice, 29 and will come forth; those who did the good *deeds* to a resurrection of life, those who committed the evil *deeds* to a resurrection of judgment. John 5:28-29 NASB

Jesus calls this servant a hypocrite, which means "one who puts on a mask and pretends to be what he is not; a dissembler in religion," or an "stage actor." [126] [127] This definition points to the antics of the Nephilim whose masks are meant to deceive but in no way will they deceive the Lord. Notice in this parable the servants were judged by what they did while the master was gone, and when he returned, there was no time for repentance. It was over.

35"Be dressed for service and keep your lamps burning, 36as though you were waiting for your master to return from the wedding feast. Then you will be ready to open the door and let him in the moment he arrives and knocks.37The servants who are ready and waiting for his return will be rewarded. I tell you the truth, he himself will seat them, put on an apron, and serve them as they sit and eat! 38He may come in the middle of the night or just before dawn. But whenever he comes, he will reward the servants who are ready.
Luke 12"35-38 NLT

# Chapter 40

## Come Out from Among Them

"Come out of her, my people, so that you will not participate in her sins and receive of her plagues; 5for her sins have piled up as high as heaven, and God has remembered her iniquities. Revelations 18:1-5 NASB

Christians may struggle with sin at times but must cry out to God for grace to walk in the victory of our Redeemer and sin no longer. When we mess up, we repent and get up, never allowing Satan victory over us.

No one who is born of God will continue to sin, because God's seed remains in him; he cannot go on sinning, because he has been born of God. 1 John 3:9

There may be friends, family, or acquaintances of the reader active in sin. Warn them, now is the hour to repent

Hear the apostles and prophets from the past who cried out to their generations to come out of Babylon. Since Babylon typifies the ways of the world and those who do not know the Lord, we must examine our lives.

> "Come out, my people, flee from Babylon. Save yourselves! Run from the LORD's fierce anger. Jeremiah 51:45 NLT
>
> With many other words he warned them; and he pleaded with them, "Save yourselves from this corrupt generation." Acts 2:40
>
> "Flee from the midst of Babylon; let everyone save his life! Be not cut off in her punishment, for this is the time of the LORD's vengeance, the repayment he is rendering her. Jeremiah 51:6 ESV

Each one of us will face death and after that judgment. We do not know our own time, but it will come (Hebrews 9:27). Will the reader be ready?

## The Narrow Door

Jesus went through the towns and villages, teaching as he went, always pressing on toward Jerusalem. ²³ Someone asked him, "Lord, will only a few be saved?" He replied, ²⁴ "Work hard to enter the narrow door to God's Kingdom, for many will try to enter but will fail. ²⁵ When the master of the house has locked the door, it will be too late. You will stand outside knocking and pleading, 'Lord, open the door for us!' But he will reply, 'I don't know you or where you come from.' 26 Then you will say, 'But we ate and drank with you, and you taught in our streets.' 27 And he will reply, 'I tell you, I don't know you or where you come from. Get away from me, all you who do evil.' Luke 13:22-27 NLT

"But keep watch on yourselves, or your hearts will become dulled by carousing, drunkenness and the worries of everyday living, and that Day will be sprung upon you suddenly like a trap! Luke 21:34 Complete Jewish Bible (CJB)

"This is all the more urgent for you know how late it is; time is running out. Wake up, for our salvation is nearer now than when we first believed." Romans 13:11 NLT

# Chapter 41

## Tree of Life, Tree of Good and Evil

> Then the LORD God said, "Behold, the man has become like one of Us, knowing good and evil; and now, he might stretch out his hand, and take also from the tree of life, and eat, and live forever -" Genesis 3:22 NLT

After the fall, man knew both good and evil. Knowing good and evil simply means to experience them both. God, who is holy, knew evil by the rebellion of Lucifer and his angels, yet desired to spare men from such knowledge. But as we know, Adam did not go along with that plan. From that point God blocked men from access to the tree of life; he would not allow sinful humans to live forever in such a state.

> Now someone may argue, "Some people have faith; others have good deeds." But I say, "How can you show me your faith if you don't have good deeds? I will show you my faith by my good deeds." James 2:18 NLT

People can live fairly good lives and have good deeds, like Cornelius, but still be cut off from the tree of eternal life (Acts 10:30-48). As already covered, a true believer in Christ possesses saving faith and deeds that work together which verifies their salvation. As a believer, one cannot have just one or the other; they must have both.

If the reader lives a good life but has not gained access to eternal life, please take a moment and consider the outcome. Eternity lasts forever; your acts of goodness do not stop judgment because of hereditary Adamic sin. The penalty for sin is death. God provided Jesus Christ as the Redeemer for all mankind, but he must be invited into your life. The first essential step must be repentance of sins.

> "...Each of you must repent of your sins and turn to God, and be baptized in the name of Jesus Christ for the forgiveness of your sins. Then you will receive the gift of the Holy Spirit. Acts 2:38 NLT

Jesus said, "In my Father's house there are many rooms and I will go and prepare a place for you" (John 14:2). If the reader has not repented of his or her sins, Satan will have successfully kept your soul for eternal punishment and away from a room in our heavenly Father's house (Matthew 25:31-46). If the reader would like to enter into a relationship with the Heavenly Father, it is time to pray.

Heavenly Father, I recognize I am a sinner. Please forgive me for all my wrongdoing. I am sorry and I want Jesus to save me. Lord Jesus you bore all sin and the punishment I deserve on the cross. I ask you to make me clean. Come into my heart and be my Lord and Savior. I choose to simply believe your word. I thank you because I ask; you answer this prayer and take me out of the Kingdom of Darkness and place me into the Kingdom of Light.

"If you confess with your mouth that Jesus is Lord and believe in your heart that God raised him from the dead, you will be saved. 10 For it is by believing in your heart that you are made right with God, and it is by confessing with your mouth that you are saved." (Romans 10:9-10 NLT).

If the reader has drifted away from the Lord and would like to repent and come back into fellowship with him, pray the above prayer and mean it.

Allow me to address the destruction of immorality. Many may still think in our day and time, there is no harm in immorality. This does not agree with the truth of God's word. Importantly, I am dealing with spiritual laws and immorality does not line up with God's commands. One's life and descendants will be affected; immorality must be stopped but better yet, never participated in at all.

> Take no part in the worthless deeds of evil and darkness; instead, expose them. Ephesians 5:11 NLT

What if a reader has children born outside the covenant of marriage and would like to bring this to God in prayer? First, God will listen, pray the above prayer and ask God for forgiveness of participation in any immorality. A child conceived outside of covenant must make his or her own decision on Lordship, but a parent can pray their child know the Lord. Become a holy role model and active in a Bible believing church.

Satan wants none to repent of immorality. What if the reader was conceived outside of a marriage covenant? Make a decision not to participant in immorality, but be vigilant, the enemy seeks to repeat this in the generations. He wants spiritual doors open to kill, steal, and destroy from the reader and his or her family.

# Conclusion

For years now, I have poured over scripture and other pertinent information to find out what the Lord needed me to know in relation to the Nephilim. In our midst are a satanic bred of humans who seek our destruction at any opportunity. They must be discerned by the Body of Christ as they continue to seduce many by their deception. The path to destroy us has not changed from the beginning, as written in Genesis chapter 6. We must endure, never giving up our faith in Jesus Christ as our Lord and Savior, the second Adam who did not fail his test.

**This is a Warning from Heaven**

Come out of sexual immorality, come out of perversion, come out of idolatry, come out of the occult, and come out of sin, while you still have time!

## Parable of 10 Virgins

"Then the kingdom of heaven will be comparable to ten virgins, who took their lamps and went out to meet the bridegroom. 2 "Five of them were foolish, and five were prudent. 3 "For when the foolish took their lamps, they took no oil with them, 4 but the prudent took oil in flasks along with their lamps. 5 "Now while the bridegroom was delaying, they all got drowsy and *began* to sleep. 6 "But at midnight there was a shout, 'Behold, the bridegroom! Come out to meet *him.*' 7 "Then all those virgins rose and trimmed their lamps. 8 "The foolish said to the prudent, 'Give us some of your oil, for our lamps are going out.' 9 "But the prudent answered, 'No, there will not be enough for us and you *too;* go instead to the dealers and buy *some* for yourselves.' 10 "And while they were going away to make the purchase, the bridegroom came, and those who were ready went in with him to the wedding feast; and the door was shut. 11 "Later the other virgins also came, saying, 'Lord, lord, open up for us.' 12 "But he answered, 'Truly I say to you, I do not know you.' 13 "Be on the alert then, for you do not know the day nor the hour. Matthew 25:1-13 NASB

12 "Behold, I am coming quickly, and My reward *is* with Me, to render to every man according to what he has done. 13 "I am the Alpha and the Omega, the first and the last, the beginning and the end." 14 Blessed are those who wash their robes, so that they may have the right to the tree of life, and may enter by the gates into the city. 15 Outside are the dogs and the sorcerers and the immoral persons and the murderers and the idolaters, and everyone who loves and practices lying. Revelations 22:12-15

"Let us rejoice and be glad and give the glory to Him, for the marriage of the Lamb has come and His bride has made herself ready." Rev 19:7 NASB

# Source Notes

1. "Dictionary and Word Search for *yatsar (Strong's 3335)*", Blue Letter Bible, 1996-2011. < http://www.blueletterbible.org/lang/lexicon/lexicon.cfm?Strongs=H3335&t=KJV (Mar 26, 2011).

2. "Dictionary and Word Search for *ganan (Strong's 1598)*", Blue Letter Bible, 1996-2011. < http://www.blueletterbible.org/lang/lexicon/Lexicon.cfm?Strongs=H1598&t=NKJV > (Sep 10, 2011).

3. "Dictionary and Word Search for '"king*" and"H4428"' in the KJV". Blue Letter Bible. 1996-2011. < http://www.blueletterbible.org/search/translationResults.cfm?Criteria=king%2A+H4428&t=KJV > (Sep17, 2011).

4. "Dictionary and Word Search for *chamac (Strong's 2555)*". Blue Letter Bible, 1996-2010. < http://www.blueletterbible.org/lang/lexicon/lexicon.cfm?Strongs=H2555&t=KJV > (Oct 17, 2010).

5. "cruelty." Free Thesaurus.org., Dictionary and Thesaurus, http://www.freethesaurus.org/dictionary/cruelty (Sep 17, 2012). 6 Ibid.

7. "oppression," Free Thesaurus.org., *Dictionary and Thesaurus*, http://www.freethesaurus.org/dictionary/ oppression (Sep 17, 2012).

8. "oppression" Roget's 21st Century Thesaurus, Third Edition. Philip Lief Group 2009. <Thesaurus.com http://thesaurus.com/browse/Oppression>. (Sep. 18, 2011).

9. Ibid.

10. "wrong," Free Thesaurus.org., Dictionary and Thesaurus, http://www.freethesaurus.org/dictionary/ oppression (Sep 17, 2012).

11. Ibid.

12. "Dictionary and Word Search for shachath (Strong's 7843)". Blue Letter Bible. 1996-2011. < http://www.blueletterbible.org/lang/lexicon/lexicon.cfm?Strongs=H7843&t=KJV > (Sept 18, 2011).

13. "deception." Webster's Revised Unabridged Dictionary (1913, 1828) *The ARTFL Project*: http://machaut.uchicago.edu/?action=search&word=deception&resource=Webster%27s&quicksearch=on (September 11, 2012).

14. Frank T. Seekins, *Hebrew Word Pictures: How does the Hebrew alphabet reveal prophetic truths* Phoenix, AZ: Living Word Pictures, 2002), 152.

15. Ibid.

16. "Dictionary and Word Search for piptō (*Strong's 4098)*". Blue Letter Bible. 1996-2010. < http://www.blueletterbible.org/lang/lexicon/lexicon.cfm?Strongs=G4098&t=KJV > (May 17, 2010).

17. John Klein and Adam Spears. Devils and Dmons and the return of the Nephilim. (Fairfax: Xulon Press, 2005), 80.

18. "Dictionary and Word Search for Abaddōn (*Strong's 3)*". Blue Letter Bible. 1996-2010.<http://www.blueletterbible.org/lang/lexicon/lexicon.cfm?strongs=G3 > (May 28, 2010).

19."Dictionary and Word Search for *Apollyōn (Strong's 623)*". Blue Letter Bible. 1996-2010. < http://www.blueletterbible.org/lang/lexicon/lexicon.cfm?Strongs=G623&t=KJV > (May 28, 2010).

20. "Dictionary and Word Search for skotos (Strongs's 4655)." Blue Letter Bible.1996-2012. < http://www.blueletterbible.org/lang/lexicon/lexicon.cfm?strongs=G4655&t=KJV> (Aug 15 2012).

21. "identical." Webster's Revised Unabridged Dictionary (1913 + 1828) *The ARTFL Project*: http://machaut.uchicago.edu/?action=search&word=identical&resource=Webster%27s&quicksearch=on (Sep 11, 2012).

18. "Dictionary and Word Search for nachash (Strong's 5172)". Blue Letter Bible. 1996-2011. < http://www.blueletterbible.org/lang/lexicon/Lexicon.cfm?Strongs=H5172&t=KJV > (Sep 12, 2011).

23. "nature." Webster's Revised Unabridged Dictionary (1913 + 1828) The ARTFL Project: http://machaut.uchicago.edu/?action=search&word=nature&resource=Webster%27s&quicksearch=on. (Sep 14, 2012).

24. "Dictionary and Word Search for patēr (Strong's 3962)". Blue Letter Bible. 1996-2010. < http://www.blueletterbible.org/lang/lexicon/lexicon.cfm?Strongs=G3962&t=KJV > (Oct 10, 2010).

25. *Book of Enoch, Ethiopic.* Richard Laurence, London, 1883. http://www.johnpratt.com/items/docs/enoch.html#Enoch_10. Chapter 40. (Sep 14, 2012).

26. Klein, John, and Adam Spears. *Devils and Demons and the Return of the Nephilim.* Fairfax: Xulon Press, 2005. 77.

27. "title." Webster's Revised Unabridged Dictionary (1913 + 1828) The ARTFL Project: http://machaut.uchicago.edu/?action=search&word=title+&resource=Webster%27s&quicksearch=on. (Jan 10, 2011).

28. "Dictionary and Word Search for *memshalah (Strong's 4475)*". Blue Letter Bible. 1996-2011. < http://www.blueletterbible.org/lang/lexicon/lexicon.cfm?Strongs=H4475&t=NIV > (Oct 31, 2011).

29. "immorality." *Webster's Revised Unabridged Dictionary (1913 + 1828)* The ARTFL Project: http://machaut.uchicago.edu/?action=search&word=

Immoral&resource=Webster%27s&quicksearch=on. (Sep 14, 2012).

30. "Dictionary and Word Search for *charah (Strong's 2734)*". Blue Letter Bible. 1996-2011. < http://www.blueletterbible.org/lang/lexicon/lexicon.cfm?Strongs=H2734&t=KJV > (Sep 27, 2011).

31. "Dictionary and Word Search for *zera`(Strong's 2233)*". Blue Letter Bible. 1996-2011. < http://www.blueletterbible.org/lang/lexicon/lexicon.cfm?Strongs=H2233&t=KJV >. (Sep 29, 2011).

32. Blue Letter Bible. "Dictionary and Word Search for *basar (Strong's 1320)*". Blue Letter Bible. 1996-2011. < http://www.blueletterbible.org/lang/lexicon/lexicon.cfm?Strongs=H1320&t=KJV >. (Sep 30, 2011).

33. Michael S. Heiser, "Deuteronomy 32:8 and the Sons of God." http://msheiser.tripod.com/ZKDT32.htm. (August 28, 2012).

34. "Dictionary and Word Search for *oikētērion (Strong's 3613)*". Blue Letter Bible. 1996-2011. < http://www.blueletterbible.org/lang/lexicon/lexicon.cfm?Strongs=G3613&t=KJV > (Oct 3, 2011).

35. "Dictionary and Word Search for 'adown (Strong's 113)". Blue Letter Bible. 1996-2011. < http://www.blueletterbible.org/lang/lexicon/lexicon.cfm?Strongs=H113&t=KJV >. (Oct 3, 2011).

36. The Book of Enoch Ethiopic. Richard Laurence, London, 1883. http://www.johnpratt.com/items/docs/enoch.html#Enoch_10. (Sep 1, 2012).

37. Proof the Book of Enoch is Scripture, http://www.scribd.com/doc/16671480/Proof-the-Book-of-Enoch-is-Scripture. (Oct 3, 2011).

38. Book of Enoch, Ethiopic. Richard Laurence, London,1883. http://www.johnpratt.com/items/docs/enoch.html #Enoch_10. (Sep 1, 2012).

39. Religions of the Ancient Mid-East. *Citizendia.* http://citizendia.org/Religions_of_the_Ancient_Near_East. (Aug 23, 2012).

40. Todd Bolen, "*Mt. Hermon*" *Bible Places*". http://www.bibleplaces.com/mthermon.htm. (Oct 27, 2011).

41. "*demigod.*" *Webster's Revised Unabridged Dictionary (1913 + 1828)* The ARTFL Project:http://machaut.uchicago.edu/?action=search&word=demigod&resource=Webster%27s&quicksearch=on. (Sep 14, 2012),

42. Smith, George. "The Chaldean Account of the Deluge", in *Transactions of the Society of Biblical Archaeology, Volumes 1-2,*. Society of Biblical Archeology; London. 1872 .213–214.

43. Klcin, John, and Adam Spears. *Devils and Demons and the Return of the Nephilim.* Fairfax: Xulon Press, 2005, 87-90.

44. Book of Enoch. Chapter 12-13, 14:3-4. http://www.johnpratt.com/items/docs/enoch.html#Enoch_1$_0$. (Aug 20, 2012).

45 "Dictionary and Word Search for *pneuma (Strong's 4151)*". Blue Letter Bible. 1996-2011. < http:// www.blueletterbible.org/lang/lexicon/lexicon.cfm? Strongs=G4151&t=KJV >. (Oct 17 2011).

46. "Dictionary and Word Search for *'Anaq (Strong's 6061)*". Blue Letter Bible. 1996-2011. < http:// www.blueletterbible.org/lang/lexicon/lexicon.cfm? Strongs=H6061&t=NIV > (Oct 17, 2011).

47. "Dictionary and Word Search for *nĕphiyl (Strong's 5303.)*." Blue Letter Bible. 1996-2011. < http:// www.blueletterbible.org/lang/lexicon/lexicon.cfm? Strongs=H5303&t=KJV >. (Oct 11, 2011).

48. Easton's Bible Dictionary (1897) "giants." World Wide Web Version "http://www.ccel.org/e/easton/ebd/ebd/T0001400.html#T0001474 (Sep 17, 2012.)

49. Blue Letter Bible. "Dictionary and Word Search for *gibbowr (Strong's 1368)*". Blue Letter Bible. 1996-2011. < http://www.blueletterbible.org/lang/lexicon/lexicon.cfm?Strongs=H1368&t=KJV >. (Oct 4, 2011).

50. Ibid.

51 "Dictionary and Word Search for *'owlam (Strong's 5769)*". Blue Letter Bible. 1996-2011. < http://www.blueletterbible.org/lang/lexicon/lexicon.cfm?Strongs=H5769&t=KJV >. (Oct 4, 2011).

52. "Dictionary and Word Search for *'alam (Strong's 5956)*". Blue Letter Bible. 1996-2011. < http://www.blueletterbible.org/lang/lexicon/Lexicon.cfm?Strongs=H5956&t=KJV >. (Oct 5, 2011).

53. "dissemble." *Dictionary.com Unabridged.* Random House, Inc. <Dictionary.com http://dictionary.reference.com/browse/dissemble>. (May 8, 2011).

54. "feller." *Roget's 21st Century Thesaurus, Third Edition.* Philip Lief Group 2009. <Thesaurus.com http://thesaurus.com/browse/feller>. (Oct. 29, 2010).

55. "Dictionary and Word Search for *'giant\* H5303'* in the KJV". Blue Letter Bible. 1996-2010. < http://www.blueletterbible.org/search/translationResults.cfm?Strongs=H5303&Criteria=giant%2A&t=KJV >. (Oct 29, 2010).

56."Dictionary and Word Search for *shem (Strong's 8034)*". Blue Letter Bible. 1996-2011. < http://www.blueletterbible.org/lang/lexicon/lexicon.cfm?Strongs=H8034&t=KJV >. (Oct 5, 2011).

57. "bully." *Dictionary.com Unabridged.* Random House, Inc. <Dictionary.com http://dictionary.reference.com/browse/bully>. (Oct 29, 2010).

58. "tyrant." Webster's Revised Unabridged Dictionary (1913 + 1828) *The ARTFL Project*: http://machaut.uchicago.edu/?action=search&word=tyrant&resource=Webster%27s&quicksearch=on. (Sep 15, 2012).

59. "tyrant." *Online Etymology Dictionary.* Douglas Harper, Historian. Dictionary.com http://dictionary.reference.com/browse/tyrant>. (Oct 04, 2011).

60. Klein, John, and Adam Spears. *Devils and Demons and the Return of the Nephilim.* Fairfax: Xulon Press, 2005. 94.

61. "abortion." *Dictionary.com Unabridged.* Random House, Inc. <Dictionary.com http://dictionary.reference.com/browse/abortion>. Mar 08, 2011.

62 "monster." *Webster's Revised Unabridged Dictionary (1913 + 1828) The ARTFL Pro*ject:http://machaut.uchicago.edu/?action=search&word=monster&resource=Webster%27s&quicksearch=on. Sep 14, 2012.

63. "*Ancient Egypt Royal Incest-The Harem and Marriage.*" Love Egypt Com http://www.love-egypt.com/royal- incest.html. (Oct 19, 2011).

64. "pervert." Dictionary.comUnbridged. Random House, Inc. <Dictionary.comhttp://dictionary.reference.com/browse/pervert>. (Nov 3, 2010).

65. "Dictionary and Word Search for `alam (*Strong's 5956*)". Blue Letter Bible. 1996-2010. < http://www.blueletterbible.org/lang/lexicon/Lexicon.cfm?Strongs=H5956&t=KJV >. (Oct 29, 2010).

66. *Book of Enoch*. Chapter 7
http://www.johnpratt.com/items/docs/enoch.html#Enoch_1
(Sep 1, 2012).

67. Ibid

68. Ibid. Chapter 8.

69. "calumny" *Webster's Revised Unabridged Dictionary (1913 + 1828)* The ARTFL Project:"http://machaut.uchicago.edu/?action=search&word=calumny&resource=Webster%27s&quicksearch=on. (Sep 15, 2012).

70. Vine, W. E., M.A. *Vine's Expository Dictionary of New Testament Words.* 1940. Print.
http://www2.mf.no/bibel/vines.html. (Aug 22, 2012).

71. Book of Enoch. Chapter 8.
http://www.johnpratt.com/items/docs/enoch.html#Enoch_10.
(Sep 1, 2012).

72. Barnes' Notes on the Bible,
http://biblecommenter.com/genesis/4-19.htm, biblos.com,
(Nov 5, 2010).

73. "Dictionary and Word Search for *kollaō (Strong's 2853)*". Blue Letter Bible. 1996-2011. < http://www.blueletterbible.org/lang/lexicon/lexicon.cfm?Strongs=G2853&t=NIV >. (Oct 16, 2011).

74. "Dictionary and Word Search for *pornē (Strong's 4204)*". Blue Letter Bible. 1996-2011. < http://www.blueletterbible.org/lang/lexicon/lexicon.cfm?Strongs=G4204&t=KJV >. (Oct 17, 2011).

75. "Dictionary and Word Search for *tsamad (Strong's 6775)*". Blue Letter Bible. 1996-2011. < http://www.blueletterbible.org/lang/lexicon/lexicon.cfm?Strongs=H6775&t=NIV >. (Oct 17, 2011).

76. "Dictionary and Word Search for *"also"'* in the NIV". Blue Letter Bible. 1996-2011. 17 Oct 2011. < http://www.blueletterbible.org/search/translationResults.cfm? Criteria=also&t=NIV >. (Oct 17, 2011).

77. Book of Enoch. "Chapter 7". "http://www.johnpratt.com/items/docs/enoch.html#Enoch_10. (Sep 1, 2012).

78. "Dictionary and Word Search for *rapha*." Blue Letter Bible. 1996-2012.
< http:// www.blueletterbible.org/lang/lexicon/lexicon.cfm? Strongs=H7497&t=KJV>. (Aug 26, 2012).

79. "Easton's 1897 Bible Dictionary." "http://www.ccel.org/e/easton/ebd/ebd3.html. (Aug 26, 2012).

80. "Dictionary and Word Search for Noach (Strong's 5146)". Blue Letter Bible. 1996-2011. < http://www.blueletterbible.org/lang/lexicon/lexicon.cfm? Strongs=H5146&t=KJV >. (Oct 20, 2011).

81. "sin," *Easton's 1897 Bible Dictionary.*" "http://www.ccel.org/e/easton/ebd/ebd3.html. > (Oct 26, 2011).

82. "Dictionary and Word Search for *akathartos (Strong's 169)*", Blue Letter Bible, 1996-2011.
http://concordances.org/greek/169.htm > < http://www.blueletterbible.org/lang/lexicon/lexicon.cfm?

Strongs=G169&t=KJV >. (Oct 21, 2011).

83. "Dictionary and Word Search for *legiōn (Strong's 3003)*". Blue Letter Bible. 1996-2011. < http://www.blueletterbible.org/lang/lexicon/lexicon.cfm? Strongs=G3003&t=KJV >. (Oct 21, 2011).

84. "Dictionary and Word Search for *kyōn (Strong's 2965)*". Blue Letter Bible. 1996-2011. < http://www.blueletterbible.org/lang/lexicon/Lexicon.cfm?

Strongs=G2965&t=KJV >. (Oct 25, 2011).

85. "Dictionary and Word Search for *daimonizomai (Strong's 1139)*". Blue Letter Bible. 1996-2011. < http://www.blueletterbible.org/lang/lexicon/lexicon.cfm?Strongs=G1139&t=NIV >. (Oct 27, 2011).

86. "possessed." Webster's Revised Unabridged Dictionary (1913 + 1828) *The ARTFL Project* http://machaut.uchicago.edu/?action=search&word=possess&resource=Webster%27s&quicksearch=on. (Sep 15, 2012).

87. Jubilees" Book of Jubilees 79-81. Sacred Texts. http://sacred-texts.com/bib/jub/jub24.htm. (Aug 18 2012).

88. "Dictionary and Word Search for *ra'ah (Strong's 7200)*". Blue Letter Bible. 1996-2011. < http://www.blueletterbible.org/lang/lexicon/lexicon.cfm?Strongs=H7200&t=NIV >. (Nov 2, 2011).

89. Blue Letter Bible. "Dictionary and Word Search for *zymē (Strong's 2219)*". Blue Letter Bible. 1996-2011. < http://www.blueletterbible.org/lang/lexicon/lexicon.cfm?Strongs=G2219&t=KJV >. (Nov 12, 2011).

90. Jubilees" *Book of Jubilees 79-81.* Sacred Texts. http://sacred-texts.com/bib/jub/jub24.htm. (Aug 18 2012).

91. Book of Enoch. "Chapter 8." http://www.johnpratt.com/items/docs/enoch.html#Enoch_10. (Sep 2, 2012).

92. Pelusi, Nando Ph.D. "All My 888 children." Psychology Today. http://www.psychologytoday.com/blog/locus-control/201008/all-my-888-children. (Aug 30, 2012).

93. Ibid.

94. Discover Magazine. "Gene Expression" http://blogs.discovermagazine.com/gnxp/2010/08/1-in-200-men-direct-descendants-of-genghis-khan/. August 30, 2012.

95. Pelusi, Nando Ph.D. "All My 888 children". *Psychology Today.* http://www.psychologytoday.com/blog/locus- control/201008/all-my-888-children. (Aug 30, 2012).

96. Ian Sample, *The Guardian.* Thursday 25 August 2011, http://www.guardian.co.uk/science/blog/2011/aug/25/neanderthal-denisovan-genes-human-immunity. (Nov 18, 2011).

97. James Owen, *National Geographic News, Neanderthals, Modern Humans Interbred*, Bone Study Suggests.http://news.nationalgeographic.com/news/2006/10/061030- neanderthals.html. (Nov 18, 2011).

98. Ibid.

99. Ker Than. "Neanderthals, Humans Interbred—First Solid DNA Evidence." *National Geographic* News, May 6, 2010. http://news.nationalgeographic.com/news/2010/05/100506-science-neanderthals-humans-mated-interbred-dna-gene/. (Sep 3, 2012).

100. Book of Jubilees. Neno. *Book of Jubilees, Chapter 7.* http://www.theforbiddenknowledge.com/hardtruth/jubilees19.htm. (Aug 19, 2012).

101. Book of Enoch. John Pratt.com. Book of Enoch, Chapter 10 http://www.johnpratt.com/items/docs/enoch.html#Enoch_10. (Aug 19, 2012).

102. Mendez, Sr. Arnold C. Noah's Ark and Early Man's Seminars. *The Wickedness of the Pre-Flood World.* http://amendez.com/NAES/Home.html. (Aug 31, 2012).

103. Ibid.

104. Stan Gooch & the Neanderthal Legacy, Oana R. Ghiocel, M.A. & Robert M. Schoch, Ph.D., New Dawn No. 125 (Mar-Apr 2011), http://www.newdawnmagazine.com. (Nov 9, 2012).

105. Ibid.

106. Ancient Wisdom. *The Role of Drugs in Prehistory.* http://www.ancient-wisdom.co.uk/prehistoricdrugs.htm. (Jul 12, 2012).

107. James Owen, National Geographic News, Neanderthals, Modern Humans Interbred, Bone Study Suggests, http://news.nationalgeographic.com/news/2006/10/061030-neanderthals.html. (Nov 11, 2011).

108. The Official King James Bible Online. *"Wisdom of Solomon Chapter 12",* http://www.kingjamesbibleonline.org/book.php?book=Wisdom+of+Solomon&chapter=12&verse=3 (Sep 18, 2012).

109. "Heyes, C. M. & Ray, E. *What is the significance of imitation in animals?* Advances in the Study of Behavior. (2000) 29, 215-245.

110. Vine, W. E. "Demon, Demoniac", Vine's Expository Dictionary of New Testament Words. Blue Letter Bible. 1940.<http://www.blueletterbible.org/Search/Dictionary/viewTopic.cfm?type=GetTopic&Topic=Demon,+Demoniac&DictList=9# Vine's>. (Nov 20, 2011).

111."consciousness." Merriam-WebsterDictionary, http://www.merriam- webster.com/dictionary/consciousness. (Nov 20, 2011).

112. "futile." *Webster's Revised Unabridged Dictionary (1913 + 1828) The ARTFL Project* http://machaut.uchicago.edu/?action=search&word=futile&resource=Webster%27s&quicksearch=on. (Sep 16, 2012.)

113. Keil and Delitzsch, *Keil and Delitzsch Biblical Commentary on the Old Testament.* Biblios.com, http://kad.biblecommenter.com/numbers/25.htm. (May 20, 2012).

114. Vine, W. E. "Repent, Repentance", Vine's Expository Dictionary of New Testament Words. Blue Letter Bible. 1940.<http://www.blueletterbible.org/Search/Dictionary/view Topic.cfm?type=GetTopic&Topic=Repent,+Repentance&DictList =9#Vine's>. (Nov 23, 2011).

115 The American Heritage® New Dictionary of Cultural Literacy, Third Edition. Houghton Mifflin Company, 2005. <Dictionary.com http://dictionary.reference.com/browse/covenant>. (Nov 27, 2011).

116. "covenant." Easton's 1897 Bible Dictionary. <Dictionary.com http://dictionary.reference.com/browse/covenant>. (Nov 27, 2011).

117. Barnes Notes on the Bible. *"Hosea 5:7."* Biblos.com. http://biblecommenter.com/hosea/5-7.htm. (Nov 29, 2011).

118. Stern, David H. Jewish New Testament Commentary: a Companion Volume to the Jewish New Testament. Clarksville, MD: Jewish New Testament Publications, 1992. Print, p. 49.

119. "Dictionary and Word Search for *sphragizō (Strong's 4972)*". Blue Letter Bible. 1996-2011. < http://www.blueletterbible.org/lang/lexicon/lexicon.cfm?Strongs=G4972&t=NIV >. (Nov 30, 2011).

120. "seal. "Webster's Revised Unabridged Dictionary (1913 + 1828) *The ARTFL Project* http://machaut.uchicago.edu/?action=search&word=seal&resource=Webster%27s&quicksearch=on. (Sep 16, 2012).

121."Dictionary and Word Search for *sphragizō (Strong's 4972)*". Blue Letter Bible. 1996-2012. < http://www.blueletterbible.org/lang/lexicon/lexicon.cfm?Strongs=G4972&t=KJV >. (Jun 20, 2012).

122. "professed." *Dictionary.com Unabridged*. Random House, Inc. <Dictionary.com http://dictionary.reference.com/browse/Professed>.(Aug 1, 2012).

123. "apostasy." *Webster's Revised Unabridged Dictionary* (1913 + 1828). *The ARTFL Pro*jecthttp://machaut.uchicago.edu/?action=search&word=apostasy&resource=Webster%27s&quicksearch=on. (Sep 16, 2012).

124. "repudiate." *Webster's Revised Unabridged Dictionary (1913+ 1828)* The ARTFL Project.http://machaut.uchicago.edu/?action=search&word=repudiate&resource=Webster%27s&quicksearch=on. (Sep 16, 2012).

125. "Dictionary and Word Search for *apostasia (Strong's 646)*". Blue Letter Bible. 1996-2012. < http://www.blueletterbible.org/lang/lexicon/lexicon.cfm?Strongs=G646&t=KJV >. (2 Aug 2012).

126. "hypocrite." *Easton's 1897 Bible Dictionary.* Third Edition, published by Thomas Nelson, 1897. http://www.ccel.org/e/easton/ebd/ebd3.html. (May 30, 2012).

127. "Dictionary and Word Search for *hypokritēs (Strong's 5273)*". Blue Letter Bible. 1996-2012. < http://www.blueletterbible.org/lang/lexicon/lexicon.cfm?Strongs=G5273&t=KJV >. (29 May 2012).

# Sources

"Ancient Egypt Royal Incest." *The Harem and Marriage.* N.p., n.d. Web. 17 Sept. 2012. <http://www.love-egypt.com/royal-incest.html>.

"Biblos.com: Search, Read, Study the Bible in Many Languages." *Biblos.com: Search, Read, Study the Bible in Many Languages.* N.p., n.d. Web. 18 Sept. 2012. <http://www.biblos.com/>.

"Blue Letter Bible - Dictionaries." *Blue Letter Bible - Dictionaries.* N.p., n.d. Web. 18 Sept. 2012. <http://cf.blueletterbible.org/Search/Dictionary/viewTopic.cfm?type=GetTopic>.

"Blue Letter Bible." *- Lexicon.* Web. 17 Sept. 2012. <http://cf.blueletterbible.org/lang/lexicon/lexicon.cfm? Strongs.

"Book of Jubilees Ch 1-9." *THE BOOK OF JUBILEES Ch 1-9.* N.p., n.d. Web. 18 Sept. 2012. <http://www.theforbiddenknowledge.com/hardtruth/jubilees1_9.htm>.

Charles, R. H., and W. O. E. Oesterley. *The Book of Enoch.* London: Society for Promoting Christian Knowledge, 1917.

"Easton's 1897 Bible Dictionary." *Easton's Bible Dictionary.* N.p., n.d. Web. 17 Sept. 2012. <http://www.ccel.org/e/easton/ebd/ebd3.html>.

"FreeThesaurus.org Dictionary and Thesaurus." *Free Thesaurus.* N.p., n.d. Web. 17 Sept. 2012. <http://www.freethesaurus.org/>.

"Genesis 4:19 Bible Commentary." *Genesis 4:19 Bible Commentary.* N.p., n.d. Web. 17 Sept. 2012. <http://biblecommenter.com/genesis/4-19.htm>.

Gordon, Cyrus. *The Ancient Near East*, 3rd Edition, Revised. W. W. Norton and Company, Inc., New York, 1965.

Heyes, C. M. & Ray, E. (2000) What is the significance of imitation in animals? Advances in the Study of Behavior.

"Proof the Book of Enoch Is Scripture." *Scribd.* N.p., n.d. Web. 17 Sept. 2012. <http://www.scribd.com/doc/16671480/Proof-the-Book-of-Enoch-is-Scripture>.

"Keil and Delitzsch Biblical Commentary on the Old Testament." *Keil and Delitzsch Biblical Commentary on the Old Testament.* N.p., n.d. Web. 18 Sept. 2012. <http://kad.biblecommenter.com/>.

Klein, John, and Adam Spears. *Devils and Demons and the Return of the Nephilim.* [S.l.]: Xulon, 2005. Print.

"Public Reference Tools - The ARTFL Project." *Public Reference Tools - The ARTFL Project.* N.p., n.d. Web. 17 Sept. 2012. <http://machaut.uchicago.edu/?action=search>.

Michael S. Heiser, "Deuteronomy 32:8 and the Sons of God." http://msheiser.tripod.com/ZKDT32.htm.

"Mount Hermon." *(BiblePlaces.com).* N.p., n.d. Web. 17 Sept. 2012. <http://www.bibleplaces.com/mthermon.htm>.

"Neandertals, Modern Humans Interbred, Bone Study Suggests." *National Geographic.* National Geographic Society, n.d. Web. 18 Sept. 2012. <http://news.nationalgeographic.com/news/2006/10/061030-neanderthals.html>.

"Noah's Ark & Early Man Seminars Noah's Ark and Early Man Seminar and Resources." *Noah's Ark & Early Man Seminars Noah's Ark and Early Man Seminar and Resources.* N.p., n.d. Web. 18 Sept. 2012. <http://amendez.com/NAES/Home.html>.

Sample, Ian. "The Guardian." *The Guardian.* Guardian News and Media, 12 Jan. 2012. Web. <http://www.guardian.co.uk/science/blog/2011/aug/25/neanderthal-denisovan-genes-human-immunity>.

Seekins, Frank T. *Hebrew Word Pictures: How Does the Hebrew Alphabet Reveal Prophetic Truths.* Phoenix, AZ: Living Word Pictures, 2002. Print.

Smith, George. "The Chaldean Account of the Deluge", in *Transactions of the Society of Biblical Archaeology, Volumes 1-2,.* Society of Biblical Archeology; London. 1872.

Than, Ker. "Neanderthals, Humans Interbred-First Solid DNA Evidence." *National Geographic.* National Geographic Society, 06 May 2010. Web. 18 Sept. 2012. <http://news.nationalgeographic.com/news/2010/05/100506-science-neanderthals-humans-mated-interbred-dna-gene/>.

"Thesaurus.com | Find Synonyms and Antonyms of Words at Thesaurus.com." *Thesaurus.com.* N.p., n.d. Web. 17 Sept. 2012. <http://thesaurus.com/>.

*Merriam-Webster.* Merriam-Webster, n.d. Web. 18 Sept. 2012. <http://www.merriam-webster.com/>.

# Author's Contact Information

V. Bryan

Dominion and Glory Ministries
1046 Church Rd., W #106-224
Southaven, MS 38671

www.endtimenephilim.com

www.ingramcontent.com/pod-product-compliance
Lightning Source LLC
Chambersburg PA
CBHW071701160426
43195CB00012B/1544